United States
Department of
Agriculture

Forest Service

Pacific Southwest
Research Station

Research Paper
PSW-RP-259
January 2009

Using HFire for Spatial Modeling of Fire in Shrublands

Seth H. Peterson, Marco E. Morais, Jean M. Carlson, Philip E. Dennison, Dar A. Roberts, Max A. Moritz, and David R. Weise

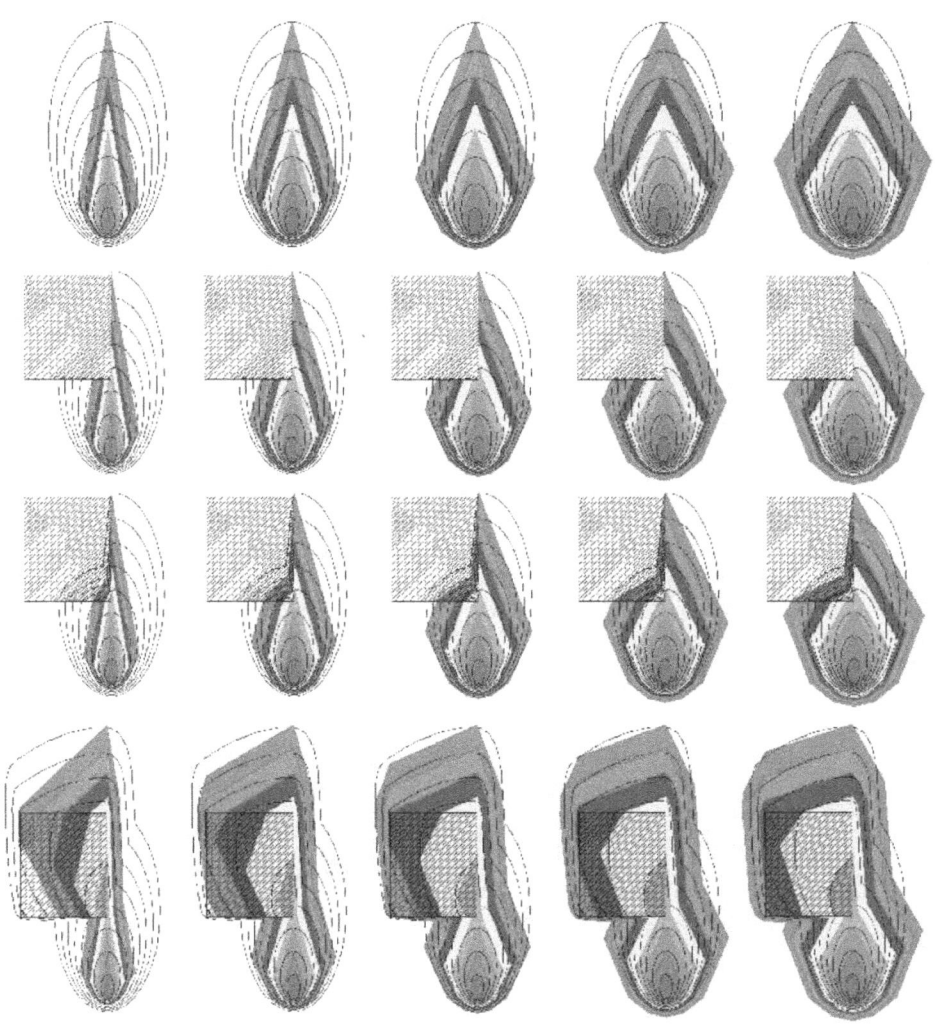

Authors

Seth H. Peterson is a Ph.D. candidate, **Jean M. Carlson** is a professor, Department of Physics, and **Dar A. Roberts** is a professor, Department of Geography, University of California, Santa Barbara, CA 93106. **Marco E. Morais** is a computer programmer, Aerospace Corporation, 2350 East El Segundo Boulevard, El Segundo, CA 90245. **Philip E. Dennison** is an assistant professor, Department of Geography, University of Utah, Salt Lake City, UT 84112. **Max A. Moritz** is an adjunct professor, Department of Environmental Science, Policy and Management, University of California, Berkeley, CA 94720. **David R. Weise** is a supervisory research forester, U.S. Department of Agriculture, Forest Service, Pacific Southwest Research Station, Forest Fire Laboratory, 4955 Canyon Crest Drive, Riverside, CA 92507.

Abstract

Peterson, Seth H.; Morais, Marco E.; Carlson, Jean M.; Dennison, Philip E.; Roberts, Dar A.; Moritz, Max A.; Weise, David R. 2008. Spatial modeling of fire in shrublands using HFire. Res. Pap. PSW-RP-259. Albany, CA: U.S. Department of Agriculture, Forest Service, Pacific Southwest Research Station. 44 p.

An efficient raster fire-spread model named HFire is introduced. HFire can simulate single-fire events or long-term fire regimes, using the same fire-spread algorithm. This paper describes the HFire algorithm, benchmarks the model using a standard set of tests developed for FARSITE, and compares historical and predicted fire spread perimeters for three southern California fires. HFire is available for download at http://firecenter.berkeley.edu/hfire.

Keywords: Fire spread model, raster, Rothermel, wildfire, southern California, chaparral.

Summary

A raster-based, spatially explicit model of surface fire spread called HFire is introduced. HFire uses the Rothermel fire spread equation to determine one-dimensional fire spread, fit to two dimensions using the solution to the fire containment problem and the empirical double ellipse formulation of Anderson. HFire borrows the idea of an adaptive time step from cell contact raster models and permits fire to spread into a cell from all neighboring cells over multiple time steps as is done in the heat accumulation approach. The model has been developed to support simulations of single-fire events and long-term fire regimes. The model implements equations for surface fire spread and is appropriate for use in grass or shrubland functional types. Model performance on a synthetic landscape, under controlled conditions was benchmarked using a standard set of tests developed initially to evaluate FARSITE. Additionally, simulations of three southern California fires spreading through heterogeneous fuels under realistic conditions showed similar performance between HFire and FARSITE, good agreement to historical reference data, and shorter model run times for HFire.

Contents

Introduction

Interest in predictive models of wildland fire spread has existed since the late 1930s, and a substantial body of related information has been published on such models (Catchpole and DeMestre 1986, Finney 1998, Fons 1946, Pitts 1991, Weber 1991, Yassemi et al. 2008). The culmination of this accumulated knowledge is encapsulated in the U.S. fire prediction system. The fire-spread predictions used by the current system are based on a semiempirical formulation first presented by Rothermel in 1972. The Rothermel equation has been implemented operationally in the form of programmable hand-held calculators in the late 1970s (Rothermel 1983), the BEHAVE minicomputer program in the middle 1980s (Andrews 1986), and the FARSITE fire-spread model in the middle 1990s (Finney 1998). FARSITE is unique because it is the first component of the national system that provides spatially explicit predictions of fire spread. In addition to the use of the Rothermel equation for modeling surface fire spread, FARSITE adds crown fire and spot fire modules for use during extreme wildfire conditions.

The fire-spread predictions used by the current system are based on a semiempirical formulation first presented by Rothermel in 1972.

HFire (a highly optimized tolerance fire-spread model) is a spatially explicit model of surface fire spread through shrubland fuels for real-time use during complex fire situations. HFire, like FARSITE, uses the Rothermel equation, but HFire uses a more computationally efficient raster-based algorithm to model fire spread in two dimensions. This allows for (1) real-time fire behavior prediction of active fires, (2) fire behavior prediction at regional spatial scales, and (3) multicentury fire regime modeling.

This paper introduces and describes the HFire fire-spread algorithm, benchmarks the model using a standard set of tests developed by Finney (1998) for FARSITE, and compares historical and predicted fire-spread perimeters for three southern California fires, for the raster (HFire) and vector (FARSITE) implementations of the Rothermel equation.

Background
Rothermel Rate-of-Spread Model

Fire-spread models can be classified according to the degree to which they are based on empirical data or physical principles (Weber 1991). Fully empirical models do not attempt to simulate the physical phenomena and instead rely on statistical correlation between variables known to influence fire spread (e.g., windspeed or slope). A very simple empirical model of fire spread might be

$$R = aU^b,$$

where the rate of fire spread, R (m/s), is the product of the windspeed, U (m/s), raised to an empirically determined power, b (unitless), and an empirically determined constant, a (unitless). Nelson and Adkins (1988) used dimensional analysis to construct a similar model from data collected during laboratory and field experiment wind-driven fires. A weakness of any fully empirical model is that predictions made for fire spread under conditions that were not explicitly tested may be unreliable.

Fully physical models differentiate among the different modes of heat transfer from burning to unburned fuel and link to the meteorological equations of motion in a way that captures the feedback between the fire and local weather conditions (Linn 1997, Linn et al. 2002). These types of models offer high fidelity, but are computationally intense and thus not suitable for use in a real-time operational setting or for multiyear simulations of fire regime (Hanson et al. 2000).

Semiempirical/semiphysical models are a blend of the two approaches. In a fully physical model, a heat-transfer calculation is used to estimate the rate of fire spread from the ratio of flux between burning and unburned fuels (Williams 1976). The Rothermel equation (1972) resembles the heat-transfer equation, but substitutes the flux components with representative empirically derived terms,

$$R = \frac{I_R \xi \ (1 + \Phi_w + \Phi_s)}{\rho_f \varepsilon \quad Q_{ig}} \ , \tag{1}$$

where I_R is the reaction intensity ($J \cdot s^{-1} \cdot m^2$), ξ is the propagating flux ratio, Φ_w is the wind factor, Φ_s is the slope factor, ρ_f is the fuel bed bulk density (kg/m^3), ε is the effective heating number, and Q_{ig} is the heat of preignition (J/kg). The Rothermel equation computes the steady-state rate of fire spread in the direction of maximum fire spread and assuming wind and slope are aligned in this direction. As a result, some other models must be used to compute the rate of fire spread in other directions and when wind and slope are not aligned with the direction of maximum spread.

Two-Dimensional Fire-Spread Modeling Approaches

Both vector and raster-based approaches have been used to model fire spread in two dimensions. The vector-based approach simulates fire spread as a continually expanding fire polygon (Anderson et al. 1982) and is the basis for the FARSITE model. Raster schemes of two-dimensional fire growth partition the modeling domain into regularly spaced square or hexagonal lattices, and fire spreads from neighboring cell to neighboring cell, using cell contact or heat accumulation methods (Ball and Guertin 1992, Berjak and Hearne 2002, Clarke et al. 1994, Frandsen and Andrews 1979, Green et al. 1990, Hargrove et al. 2000, Kourtz and O'Regan 1971, Yassemi et al. 2008).

In the vector approach to modeling fire spread, the fire perimeter at any point in time is represented by an infinitely thin arc consisting of a set of *n* coordinate pairs, known as vertices, in a Cartesian plane. The maximum rate of spread is computed at each vertex, and empirical relationships developed by Anderson (1983) are used to predict the elliptical shape of fire spread from the maximum rate of fire spread and the local wind and slope conditions. The convex hull about the *n* fire-prediction ellipses defines the perimeter of the fire for the next time step. The number of coordinate pairs, *n*, relative to the length of the perimeter, *l*, dictates the spatial resolution of the predicted fire spread; referred to as "perimeter resolution" in FARSITE.

One of the weaknesses of the vector approach is the difficulty in choosing an appropriate perimeter resolution. Clarke et al. (1994) observed from historical fire scars that fire perimeter length is strongly dependent upon scale, and this suggests a uniform perimeter resolution may not be appropriate. Another weakness of the vector approach is the need for a computationally expensive convex hull fire-spread perimeter generation procedure (Richards 1990) at the end of each time step in order to resolve fire crossovers and unburned islands. In a critical evaluation of a fire-spread model implementing Huygens' Principle, French et al. (1990) found that the model performance suffered under increasingly heterogeneous conditions. Despite this, the most widely used fire-spread models in the United States (FARSITE) (Finney 1998), Canada (Prometheus) (Prometheus 2008), and Australia (SiroFire) (Coleman and Sullivan 1996) all use the vector approach to modeling fire spread.

Green (1983) identified two main approaches to determining fire spread in a raster domain: heat accumulation and cell contact. The cell contact approach, used by Kourtz and O'Regan (1971), Frandsen and Andrews (1979), and Green et al. (1990), is consistent with an interpretation of fire spread as a series of discontinuous ignitions spanning the length of an individual cell. The strength of this approach is that it is extremely computationally efficient because the simulation clock increments in nonuniform intervals based on the amount of time required to spread into an adjacent cell; this is sometimes referred to as the time-of-arrival (TOA) of the fire perimeter. This eliminates the redundant computations that are made when operating with a uniform time step. The weakness of the contact approach is that events are generated based only upon the influence of the single fastest spreading neighbor, and fire spread into a cell that is the cumulative effect of multiple neighboring cells or prior heating is neglected (Green 1983).

The heat accumulation approach to raster fire spread mitigates the fundamental weakness of the cell contact approach by enabling the rate of spread of fire into a cell to be the sum of the contribution of neighboring ignited cells during prior time steps (Green 1983). The heat accumulation model iterates over fixed time intervals, known as the time step, visiting every cell in the simulation domain and tabulating the quantity of heat received by that cell from all of its neighbors. After receiving some threshold quantity of heat, a cell is considered ignited and begins delivering heat to neighboring cells. Although the phrase "heat accumulation" suggests that there is a physical basis for the method used to describe the ability of a cell to absorb and emit heat, all implementations to date have used fully empirical or semiempirical/semiphysical models of fire spread as surrogates for the physical properties and mechanisms of fire spread (Green et al. 1990). French et al. (1990) empirically evaluated the performance of a heat accumulation model (Green 1983) and found that it was more computationally intensive than the cell contact approach because of the relatively small elapsed time step required to capture rapid fire spread. However, the added cost appeared worthwhile because the fire-spread perimeters produced from the heat accumulation model were less distorted in comparison to the cell contact models. Most recent raster fire-spread models use the heat accumulation approach (Anderson et al. 2007, Ball and Guertin 1992, Berjak and Hearne 2002, Clarke et al. 1994, Hargrove et al. 2000, Vasconcelos and Guertin 1992, Yassemi et al. 2008). Yassemi et al. (2008) performed an analysis similar to our analysis. They compared a raster and a vector (Prometheus) implementation of the semiempirical fire-spread algorithm used by government agencies in Canada, finding the best agreement at high windspeeds.

The HFire Model

Model Description

HFire (Morais 2001) is a raster model of surface fire spread based on the Rothermel (1972) fire-spread equation and the empirical double ellipse formulation of Anderson (1983). HFire blends the strengths of the contact-based and heat accumulation raster fire-spread approaches; it borrows the idea of an adaptive time step from the cell contact models and permits fire to spread into a cell from all neighboring cells over multiple time steps as is done in the heat accumulation approach. A state machine is used to track the movement of the fire through the cells in the simulation domain.

The model can be run in two modes, simulating single-fire events or long-term fire regimes. The fire-spread algorithm used in both modes of the operation is the same, resulting in no loss of fidelity whether the model is being run for a single event or for a scenario spanning several centuries. Single-event simulations driven by historical or predicted data are completely deterministic. Although not

HFire is a raster model of surface fire spread based on the Rothermel fire-spread equation and the empirical double ellipse formulation of Anderson.

discussed in this paper, the model can be used for multiyear simulations of fire regime (many hundreds of years) featuring stochastic historical weather patterns, ignition frequency and location, simulated Santa Ana wind events, and dynamic fuels regrowth (Moritz et al. 2005). Hfire has also been used to examine sensitivity to weather inputs (Clark et al., in press) and the effectiveness of fire suppression (Ntaimo et al. 2004).

Model Inputs

HFire model inputs can be subdivided into three groups: (1) fuel variables, (2) terrain variables, and (3) environmental variables (table 1).

Table 1—Variables required for predicting fire spread using HFire

Variable	Type	Units
Fuel load	Fuel	kg/m^2
Surface area to volume (σ)	Fuel	m^2/m^3
Heat content	Fuel	J/kg
Total silica content	Fuel	Percent
Effective silica content	Fuel	Percent
Fuel bed depth	Fuel	m
Moisture of extinction	Fuel	Percent
Elevation	Terrain	m
Slope	Terrain	Percent
Aspect	Terrain	Degrees
Dead fuel moisture	Environmental	Percent
Live fuel moisture	Environmental	Percent
Windspeed	Environmental	m/s
Wind direction	Environmental	Degrees

Fuel variables require a value for each of the following size classes: dead 1-hour (<0.635 cm diameter), dead 10-hour (0.635 to 2.54 cm diameter), dead 100-hour (2.54 to 7.62 cm diameter), live herbaceous, and live woody fuels.

Fuel variables—

Fuels are described using the parameter sets (fuel models) for the Rothermel model developed by Albini (1976). The 13 Northern Forest Fire Laboratory (NFFL) standard fuel models (Albini 1976) or user-defined custom fuel models (Burgan and Rothermel 1984) can be used in HFire. A look-up table applied to the fuel model map provides fuel information across the landscape. Because the Rothermel equation assumes a homogeneous fuel bed, a method of averaging the collections of fuel particles used by the fuel modeling system is required. HFire uses the surface-area-to-volume weighting scheme described by Rothermel (1972) to synthesize the fuel particle attributes into a single-characteristic value of the fuel bed. Although some fuel variables such as fuel load and depth vary annually owing to disturbance and seral stage, the change in these properties within a single year is small enough to justify holding them constant during a year of simulation time. Fuel moisture varies on a daily basis (dead) or seasonal basis (live) and is treated as an environmental variable by the model.

Terrain variables—
The terrain variables used by the model (elevation, slope, and aspect) are typically computed from a digital elevation model (DEM) using a geographic information system (GIS). These are held constant for the duration of single-event and multiyear simulations.

Environmental variables—
The environmental variables used by the model can vary in both time and space. Inputs can be specified to a minimum resolution of 1 hour,[1] which is common for windspeed, wind azimuth, and dead fuel moisture. This constraint does not reflect a limitation of the internal simulation clock but is imposed because estimates for these parameters are commonly taken from Remote Automated Weather Stations (RAWS) that report data in 1-hour intervals. Live fuel moisture changes more slowly; it is measured in the field at 2-week intervals but can be input at any resolution up to hourly. The inputs can be constant on the landscape or maps of values. Spatially varying environmental inputs can be specified at a spatial resolution different from that of the terrain and fuels variables and up to a minimum temporal resolution of 1 hour. Diagnostic wind models are a potential source for spatially varying weather inputs (Butler et al. 2006), and remote sensing is a potential source for live fuel moisture maps (Dennison et al. 2003, 2005; Peterson et al., in press; Roberts et al. 2006).

HFire assumes windspeed and direction data are measured at the conventional reference height for RAWS stations in the United States, 6.1 m above the top of the fuel bed. HFire uses an approximation[2] to the logarithmic reduction formula given by Albini and Baughman (1979) to compute the windspeed experienced at mid-flame from the windspeed measured at the reference height,

---

[1] This restriction will be relaxed in future versions of HFire to allow time tagged inputs specified at any resolution.

[2] There is a slight discrepancy between the mid-flame windspeed computed from Albini and Baughman (1979) and the mid-flame windspeed computed using BEHAVEPlus. The windspeed adjustment factor (WAF) used in BEHAVEPlus (WAF_{BHP}) can be recovered from the Albini and Baughman equation (WAF_{AB79}) using the following linear equation: $WAF_{BHP} = WAF_{AB79} * 1.371817779 + 0.046171831$. The results reported in this paper use the WAF from BEHAVEPlus.

$$U_{mid} = \frac{U_{ref}}{\ln\left[\dfrac{h_{ref} + (0.36\,h_{mid})}{0.13\,h_{mid}}\right]} \quad,$$

where U_{mid} is the mid-flame windspeed (m/s), U_{ref} is the windspeed measured at the reference height (m/s), h_{ref} is the reference height (m), and h_{mid} is the mid-flame height (m). In HFire, the mid-flame height, h_{mid}, is assumed to be equal to twice the fuel bed depth. Although others have suggested that a logarithmic windspeed reduction profile may be less accurate during periods of local atmospheric instability (Beer 1990) and during nighttime conditions (Rothermel et al. 1986), HFire uses this adjustment throughout the duration of the simulation.

Two-Dimensional Fire Spread

There is widespread agreement that fire spread under steady homogeneous conditions and in the presence of wind and topography roughly approximates an expanding ellipse (Anderson 1983, Green 1983). Anderson (1983) described fire spread as a double ellipse, which allows for different equations for the forward and backward spreading ellipses. The length-to-width ratio of the ellipses is a function of the mid-flame windspeed.

Since Rothermel's original fire-spread equation assumes that the wind is aligned directly with slope, the effect of cross-slope winds must be taken into account. HFire uses the technique defined in Rothermel (1983: fig. IV-8) to compute the cross-slope rate of spread vector by adding two rate-of-spread vectors, one computed using the observed winds without slope and another using the slope and no wind. The windspeed in the direction of the cross-slope rate of spread vector, termed the effective windspeed, U_{eff} (m/s), is used to compute the length-to-width ratio of an ellipse (Rothermel 1991: equation [9]),

$$\frac{L}{W} = 1 + 0.5592\,k U_{eff} \tag{2}$$

where L is equal to the length (m) and W is equal to the width (m) of the predicted elliptical dimensions. The coefficient k is an addition to Rothermel's (1991) equation[3] that we have included in HFire and termed the ellipse adjustment factor (EAF). The EAF is included in HFire as a correction factor for grid-induced

---

[3] Equation 5 in Rothermel (1991) is a linearization of an exponential function suggested by Andrews (1983) where U is given in mi/hr. Equation 2 in this paper uses U in m/s and as a result the coefficient 0.25 in mi hr^{-1} has been divided by (1609.344 m/3600s) in order for L and W to remain unitless.

effects associated with the raster-based algorithm. The raster-based algorithm generally produces narrower, more angular fire shapes than FARSITE when $k = 1.0$ (i.e., no EAF correction); values of k less than 1.0 widen the fire front for HFire. The rationale for the EAF is explained in more detail following equation (3).

Albini and Chase (1980) provided a formula (equation 8) for determining the eccentricity of an ellipse, E, such that $0 < E < 1$ and using the length, L, and width, W:

$$E = \frac{\sqrt{\left(\frac{L}{W}\right)^2 - 1}}{\left(\frac{L}{W}\right)} .$$

Given the predicted eccentricity, E, of the fire calculated from the effective windspeed and the rate of maximum fire spread calculated from the Rothermel equation, R_{max}, the solution to the fire containment problem (Albini and Chase 1980) provides the rate of fire spread at arbitrary angles from the maximum:

$$R_\theta = R_{max} \frac{(1 - E)}{(1 - E \cos\theta)} , \tag{3}$$

where R_θ is the rate of fire spread (m/s), at some angle θ (degrees), from the direction of the maximum rate of fire spread. The derivative of equation (3) with respect to the angle, θ, is largest at small angles, $0° < \theta < \pm45°$. For example, the eccentricity for typical length-to-width ratios (12:1 to 3:1) is on the order of 0.9, and for this value, R_{45} is reduced to 27 percent of R_0 using equation (3). Hence, for a raster model allowing fire spread to eight neighbors, where the values of the angle θ in equation (3) are restricted to multiples of 45° in the range [-180°, 180°], the region from 0° to ±45° is undersampled and poorly approximates the true shape of the function. As a result, the shape of the heading portion of the fire is angular rather than rounded, in comparison to a vector model (Ball and Guertin 1992, French et al. 1990).

The EAF is introduced to compensate for this distortion. The effect of the EAF on predicted fire shapes on a landscape with flat terrain, homogeneous fuels, and under uniform wind conditions is shown in figure 1. In all cases, the distance spread in the direction of the maximum rate of fire spread (from the ignition point to the fire front) is unchanged, but the fire front is less pointed (EAF < 1.0) than the raster realization of Anderson's (1983) standard fire-spread ellipse (EAF = 1.0). For example, for an effective windspeed of 5 m/s, R_{45} is reduced to 25 percent of R_0 with EAF = 0.5 and to 11 percent with EAF = 1.0. When conditions are less simplified, the heading portion of the fire will become more blunted as the direction of the maximum rate of fire spread changes, and an EAF closer to 1.0 can be used.

Recommendations for setting the EAF appropriately are made in the "Discussion" section.

In any three-by-three neighborhood of cells, a fire located at the center of the neighborhood has the potential of spreading to all eight adjacent neighbors. The fire-spread distance in the direction of a neighboring cell located at some angle θ, in degrees, from the cell center during the nth iteration $d_{\theta,n}$ is equal to the rate of fire spread in the direction of the neighbor during the nth iteration $R_{\theta,n}$ multiplied by the duration of the time step t_n:

$$d_{\theta,n} = R_{\theta,n}\, t_n \ .$$

Under homogeneous conditions, an eight-sided figure will always emerge because the underlying raster provides eight degrees of freedom.

Adaptive Time Step

The cell size, Δd, provides a lower limit on the distance between adjacent cells in the simulation. The terrain distance, d_{xyz}, is necessary for tracking fire spread parallel to the ground and is computed from a pair of cells in three-dimensional Cartesian space $\{x_1, y_1, z_1\}$ and $\{x_2, y_2, z_2\}$ as:

$$d_{xyz} = \sqrt{\left(x_1 - x_2\right)^2 + \left(y_1 - y_2\right)^2 + \left(z_1 - z_2\right)^2} \ .$$

The terrain distance between adjacent cells at the same elevation and connected via one of the four cardinal directions, 0 (north), 90 (east), 180 (south), or 270 (west) degrees, will always be equal to or longer than the cell size. Similarly, the terrain distance between cell centers connected by a diagonal will always be longer than the cell size. Thus, the cell size, Δd, divided by the maximum rate of fire spread at all cells in the simulation domain during the nth iteration, max $|R_{max,n}|$, yields the minimum amount of time, in seconds, that can occur in the simulation before the fire may have traveled from one cell center to another during a single time step. This provides the basis[4] for the size of the time step used during the nth iteration, t_n:

$$t_n = \frac{\Delta d}{\max | R_{max,n}|} \ . \tag{4}$$

Because the size of the time step will vary with fire behavior, incrementing more slowly when fire spread is rapid and vice-versa, this is referred to as an adaptive time step.

---

[4] The distance past a neighboring cell center that a fire spreads during a single iteration is termed the "slop over." HFire properly handles "slop over," but an attempt is made to minimize the frequency with which it occurs by scaling the time step computed using equation 4 by 0.25. More details are provided in the section on modeling fire spread at subcell resolutions.

Modeling Fire Spread at Subcell Resolutions

Given a method for computing the rate of fire spread in any direction and for determining an appropriate time step from the fastest spreading component of the fire, a state machine is used to track the movement of the fire through the cells in the simulation domain. At any instant in the simulation, all cells in the simulation domain are assigned one of four possible states.

- Cell is **unburnable** [U].
- Cell is flammable, but **not currently ignited** [N].
- Cell is flammable and is **ignited**, but fuel is not yet consumed [I].
- All fuel in cell has been **consumed** by the fire [C].

At the start of the simulation, all cells are in the unburnable [U] or not-currently-ignited [N] states. Unburnable cells [U] correspond to areas without the potential to burn, such as rock outcrops and water bodies, including the ocean, lakes, and perennial streams. There are no transitions to or from the unburnable state to any of the other three states.

During the simulation, there are two possible events that can result in the transition of a cell from the not currently ignited state [N] to the ignited state [I]. The first type of transition event is an independent ignition that represents a new fire. Independent ignitions can be specified by the user in two ways. For single-event simulations, the user typically supplies a file containing the coordinates of cells that will be ignited [I] at the start of the first iteration in the simulation. For multiyear simulations, the user specifies two types of ignition probabilities: an overall temporal frequency for ignitions and a surface containing the relative probability of ignition for each cell. Ignitions occur stochastically in time and space.

The second type of transition event occurs when a fire spreads into the cell from an adjacent cell. HFire implements fire spread as follows. The simulation maintains a list of all cells that are in the ignited state [I]. Two arrays are associated with each element of this list. The first array is used to accumulate the distance over multiple time steps that the fire has traveled in each of the eight possible directions. The second array is used to store the terrain distance, d_{xyz}, between adjacent cells in each direction. When the accumulated distance in a direction exceeds the terrain distance in that direction, then the adjacent cell in that direction is transitioned from the not ignited state [N] to the ignited state [I]. Any excess distance, termed "slop over," is applied to the array of accumulated distances for the newly ignited cell in the direction of fire spread.

During the simulation, there are two possible events that can result in the transition of a cell from the ignited state [I] to the consumed state [C]. The first type of transition event is triggered when the eight neighbors of a cell are in the ignited state [I] or unburnable state [U]. Cells in this configuration are typically located in the interior portions of an expanding fire. This is not meant to imply that cells in the consumed state [C] are not undergoing postfrontal combustion, only that the energy released from these cells no longer contributes to the forward rate of spread of the fire. The second type of transition event occurs when a fire is extinguished; this is important for the multiyear model runs.

Fire does not burn in a cell indefinitely. Fire extinction refers to the transition of a cell from the ignited state [I] to the not-ignited state [N] or from the ignited state [I] to the consumed state [C]. The Rothermel model given in equation (1) does not describe the conditions under which a fire is extinguished. As a result, the simulation uses a few additional heuristics to trigger extinction. First, a cell in the ignited state [I] that has burned longer than a user-specified threshold without propagating to all adjacent burnable neighbors will trigger an extinction transition; this is implemented in the simulation by tracking the time since each cell was ignited. Second, a cell in the ignited state [I] with a maximum rate of fire spread that falls below a user-specified threshold will trigger an extinction transition. In both cases, the user controls whether all extinction transitions will go from ignited [I] to not ignited [N] or from ignited [I] to consumed [C].

Methods

In this section, we describe two sets of numerical simulations to evaluate the performance of HFire. First, a series of benchmarks on synthetic, homogeneous landscapes under simplified burning conditions were performed, following the initial landmark validation of the FARSITE implementation of the Rothermel equation (Finney 1998). For all of the HFire simulations, we ran comparison simulations with FARSITE, using the same inputs, enabling a direct comparison of the results. Second, simulations of three historical fires with mapped topography and vegetation and measured weather were performed, and HFire perimeters were compared to FARSITE perimeters and reference fire perimeters.

All tests were performed with the same inputs, with the exception of dead fuel moisture, which is input differently for HFire and FARSITE. HFire uses hourly 10-hour dead fuel moisture data from RAWS stations, and the 1-hour and 100-hour dead fuel moistures are determined from the 10-hour values ± a user-defined constant. For FARSITE 1-, 10-, and 100-hour dead fuel moistures are initialized at the beginning of the simulation period and are modified using a sinusoidal function whose shape is dictated by air temperature and humidity.

For all of the HFire simulations, we ran comparison simulations with FARSITE, using the same inputs, enabling a direct comparison of the results.

FARSITE contains modules for predicting fire spread in grassland, shrubland, and forested landscapes, whereas HFire is designed for surface fire in chaparral landscapes comprising grasslands and shrublands only. FARSITE modules for forested landscapes that allow for spotting and crown fires are not applicable. In addition, the FARSITE fire acceleration module is disabled so that a comparison between the two model implementations of the Rothermel equation could be performed.

Agreement between HFire- and FARSITE-modeled fire perimeters, as well as between modeled and historical fire perimeters, was assessed using the Sørensen metric. The Sørensen metric (Greig-Smith 1983, Perry et al. 1999) measures agreement between two areas:

$$S = \frac{2a}{(2a + b + c)} \quad ,$$

where a is the intersection of the area burned in the two models, b is the area burned by model A but not model B, and c the area burned by model B but not model A. A value of $S = 1.0$ indicates perfect agreement. All calculations are performed on cumulative area burned for an individual fire. Perry et al. (1999) used the Sørensen metric to assess the accuracy of a simulation of the 1995 Cass Fire in New Zealand.

Synthetic Landscape Tests

A series of simple, controlled tests were designed by Finney (1998) to illustrate the response of the FARSITE fire-spread model to the primary factors affecting fire spread. These factors include windspeed, wind direction, slope, fuel type, and fuel transitions. They are varied individually and in pairs under otherwise uniform conditions to illustrate model behavior under idealized, controlled conditions. To evaluate HFire, we replicated the burning conditions used by Finney (1998) to test the FARSITE model.

In all of the tests, fuel moisture was held constant, spatial resolution was 10 m, and perimeters were output at hourly time steps. Unless otherwise specified, wind direction was from 180 degrees; values of EAF tested were 1, 0.66, 0.5, 0.4, and 0.33; fuel model 15, a custom fuel model for mature chamise chaparral (Weise and Regelbrugge 1997), was used, and the terrain was flat.

Test of different windspeeds —
This test isolates the effects of windspeed and the EAF. Twenty-one separate HFire simulations were run. Windspeed ranged from 0 to 20 m/s, in increments of 5 m/s. Five values of EAF were tested, except for the 0 m/s windspeed case, where EAF

A series of simple, controlled tests were designed by Finney (1998) to illustrate the response of the FARSITE fire-spread model to the primary factors affecting fire spread.

has no effect. For the zero m/s windspeed simulations, Fuel Model 1, grassland, was used to increase rate of spread, so the figure is less pixilated.

Test of time varying wind direction —

This test isolates the effect of varying wind direction and EAF. Thirty HFire simulations were run, the five values of EAF were tested with six wind azimuths: winds having a constant azimuth of 180 degrees and five different wind azimuth scenarios, listed in table 2. For the first four scenarios, the wind direction is periodically and deterministically varied by fixed increments about the 180-degree average. In the last scenario, the wind direction switches between due north and due south. Windspeed was 5 m/s for all runs.

Table 2—Scenarios for alternating wind azimuth condition tests

Scenario[a]	Hour								
	0	1	2	3	4	5	6	7	8
	Degrees								
1	180	190	170	185	175	180	190	170	180
2	180	210	150	195	165	180	210	150	180
3	200	220	170	210	130	190	220	140	180
4	180	225	135	225	135	225	135	180	180
5	180	360	180	360	180	360	180	360	180

[a] The first four scenarios involve perturbations about 180 degrees, the last involves alternating wind directions.

Test of different windspeeds and slopes, with up-slope winds —

This test combines the effects of changing both windspeed and slope. Twenty-four HFire and FARSITE simulations were run, with slopes (rise over run) of 0, 20, 40, 60, 80, and 100 percent and constant upslope windspeeds of 0, 2.5, 5, and 7.5 m/s. A fire burning uphill spreads faster as the heat from the fire front preheats the adjacent fuel, driving off vegetation moisture, reducing the energy required to raise the temperature of the fuel to ignition. HFire was run with the EAF set to 0.5.

Test of different slopes and cross-slope winds —

This test combines the effects of changing slope and temporally varying wind direction. It is similar to the previous test with different windspeeds and slopes, with the modification that the wind direction is cross-slope. We tested two wind direction scenarios: winds from 270 degrees and winds from 270 degrees systematically perturbed ± 20 degrees. Only 7.5 m/s windspeed model runs are presented. HFire was run with the EAF set to 0.5.

Test of different fuel model transitions —

This test isolates the effects of fuel model transitions and the EAF. Twenty HFire simulations were run with five values for the EAF and four landscape scenarios: a landscape solely comprising Fuel Model 15, and Fuel Model 15 with an inset block of three different fuel models (unburnable; a synthetic fuel model based on Fuel Model 15 but with reduced fine fuel loads so that it burns more slowly than Fuel Model 15; and Fuel Model 1, grassland, which results in faster fire spread). Wind-speed was 7 m/s.

Historical Fires

**The initial stages
of three historical
chaparral fires
were simulated.**

This section tests agreement between HFire, FARSITE, and reference fire perimeters when wind, fuels, and terrain vary under actual burning conditions. The initial stages of three historical chaparral fires were simulated. The Day Fire burned slowly for a month in southern California in 2006. The Simi Fire was part of a complex of fires burning under extreme Santa Ana conditions in southern California in late October of 2003. The Calabasas Fire was a short-lived Santa Ana wind-driven event. The initial stages of the Day Fire are presented first to demonstrate a relatively simple scenario involving low windspeeds that is intermediate in complexity between the synthetic landscapes and the more complex Simi and Calabasas Fires.

Two types of comparisons are made in this section: model to model, and both HFire and FARSITE models to measured perimeters, all at hourly time steps. Model-to-model comparisons under realistic burning conditions serve as further benchmarks of HFire. Comparisons between modeled and reference perimeters build understanding and gain confidence. The accuracy of modeled perimeters is limited by the underlying semiempirical/semiphysical nature of the Rother-mel equation, the spatial resolution of the landscape variables, and the temporal (hourly) and spatial (point) resolution of the wind data. Furthermore, historical fire suppression information is often not available or available in a way that is easily incorporated into the models. Finally, the accuracy of the reference historical fire perimeters differs and may not be the absolute standard needed. Hence, the primary benefit of the models vs. reality comparisons lies in developing a general understanding of fire modeling, and defining future directions for model refinement to improve model accuracy and predictive power.

Day Fire —

The Day Fire was reported at 1355 hours on 4 September 2006 and was contained on 2 October 2006. It burned 65 871 ha, and cost $73.5 million to suppress. The fire initially spread slowly, burning only 5000 ha by 9 September. Major wind-driven runs occurred on the 12th, 16th through 19th, 22nd through 24th, and 27th of September.

Only the first 58 hours of burning (1400 hours 4 September to 2300 hours 6 September) are simulated as both fire-spread models dramatically overpredict initial fire growth, owing to effective fire suppression efforts at the initial stages of the actual event.

The Day Fire burned through a southern California chaparral/coastal sage scrub (CSS) mosaic. The state of California Fire and Resource Assessment Program (FRAP) map was used to determine fuel models. Two different sets of fuel models were used to characterize the vegetation (table 3): the fuel models developed by Anderson (1983), formally called the NFFL models; and custom fuel models that were specifically developed for chaparral, the Riverside Fire Lab (RFL) fuel models (Weise and Regelbrugge 1997). The 1-, 10-, and 100-hour fuel size classes of table 3 correspond to <¼-, ¼- to 1-, and 1- to 3-in diameter woody material, and are based on how quickly dead fuel moisture responds to changes in atmospheric relative humidity.

Table 3—Biomass and fuel bed depth for the fuel models used in this study

		Fuel biomass					
		Dead			Live		
Fuel model	Fuel model description	1-hr	10-hr	100-hr	Herbaceous	Woody	Fuel bed depth
		- - - - - - - - - - - - - - - - *Mg/ha* - - - - - - - - - - - - - - -					*Centimeters*
NFFL 1	Grass	1.66	0	0	0	0	30.48
NFFL 2	Savana	4.49	2.25	1.12	0	1.12	30.48
NFFL 4	Shrub	11.25	9.01	4.49	0	11.25	182.88
NFFL 5	Shrub	2.25	1.12	0	0	4.49	60.96
NFFL 6	Shrub	3.37	5.61	4.49	0	0	76.20
NFFL 8	Timber	3.37	2.25	5.61	0	0	6.10
NFFL 10	Timber	6.76	4.49	11.25	0	4.49	30.48
RFL 15	Old chamise	4.48	6.73	2.24	1.12	4.48	91.44
RFL 16	Ceanothus	5.04	10.76	4.04	6.73	6.28	182.88
RFL 18	Sagebrush/buckwheat	12.33	1.79	0.22	1.68	5.6	91.44
FARSITE 99	Unburnable	0	0	0	0	0	0

Size classes are 1-hour (<0.635 cm diameter), 10-hour (0.635-2.54 cm diameter), 100-hour (2.54-7.62 cm diameter).
NFFL= Northern Forest Fire Laboratory.
RFL= Riverside Fire Laboratory.

The 30-m FRAP fuels map uses NFFL fuel models; however, the fuel models for shrubs were changed to the RFL chaparral fuel models for this analysis. NFFL Fuel Model 4 was converted to RFL 16 (*Ceanothus* chaparral), NFFL 6 to RFL 15 (mature chamise chaparral), and NFFL 5 to RFL 18 (CSS). Fuel Models 28, 98, 15, and 97, which represent urban, water, desert, and irrigated agriculture, respectively, were reclassified to Fuel Model 99, the designated number for unburnable cells. Topographic variables were derived from a 30-m U.S. Geological Survey (USGS) DEM. Slope and aspect were derived using standard techniques.

The weather data were obtained from the Cheeseboro, California, RAWS, which is located 48 km south of the final fire extent. The RAWS closer to the fire were not used because data were either missing or noisy. The RAWS data consist of daily precipitation, maximum/minimum temperature, maximum/minimum humidity, timing of maximum and minimum temperatures (hourly values are interpolated by FARSITE), and elevation of the weather station (needed to interpolate weather variables across the landscape, using environmental lapse rates). Live fuel moisture during the simulation was held constant at a value of 60-percent of ovendry weight (ODW) for live herbaceous material and for live woody material. Live fuel moisture in chaparral in the fall drops to the annual minimum value, which is on the order of 60 percent (Countryman and Dean 1979, Roberts et al. 2006).

Accuracy was assessed using a perimeter derived from the MODIS active fire product, which uses data from both the Aqua and Terra satellites. It is produced four times a day, at 1-km cell resolution. The reference perimeter was generated by calculating a convex hull polygon about the set of all active fire cells from the MODIS active fire product (current and past) for the Day Fire as of 2300 hours on 6 September.

Simi Fire —

The Simi Fire burned from October 25 to November 5, 2003, consumed 44 000 ha, destroyed 315 structures, and cost approximately $10 million to suppress. It was a Santa Ana wind-driven fire, which exhibited rapid westward growth on the 26th of October owing to high windspeeds. The first 34 hours of the fire were simulated, from 1300 hours on 25 October to 2300 hours on 26 October. The Simi Fire was chosen for simulation because it is representative of fires in chaparral, experiencing high windspeeds and high rates of spread.

The Simi Fire burned through a southern California chaparral/grassland mosaic. The state of California FRAP map was used to determine fuel models as described above for the Day Fire. Topographic variables were derived from a 30-m USGS DEM; slope and aspect were derived using standard techniques. Weather data were obtained from the Cheeseboro, California, RAWS Station, located 8 km south of the central portion of the final fire extent.

Accuracy was assessed using perimeters derived from the MODIS active fire product. Convex hull polygons were generated from the set of all active fire cells (current and past) for each time step. These polygons were then clipped using the official final fire perimeter from the California Department of Forestry and Fire Prevention (CDF) to remove the presence of false positives in the MODIS product.

The Simi Fire was chosen for simulation because it is representative of fires in chaparral, experiencing high windspeeds and high rates of spread.

Calabasas Fire —

The 1996 Calabasas Fire burned 5159 ha in the Santa Monica Mountains, California. The Calabasas Fire was chosen for simulation based on the availability of hourly perimeter data for the fire, and availability of remote sensing data for mapping prefire fuels. The Calabasas Fire was a Santa Ana wind-driven event, typical of conditions under which the majority of burning takes place in shrublands of southern California (Keeley et al. 1999, Moritz et al. 2004). The fire was actively spreading from the time it started along U.S. Highway 101 on October 21, 1996, at approximately 1100 hours Pacific Daylight Time until contained on the morning of October 22.

The northern and southern portions of the Calabasas Fire were modeled separately for comparison to the helicopter-based reference perimeters. The northern portion of the fire occurred between 1100 and 1500 hours. A second simulation period, from 1500 to 2200 hours, was also examined as a spot fire over Malibu Canyon Road acted as a point source for a "new" fire.

Historical windspeed, wind direction, and dead fuel moisture data during the fire are available on an hourly basis from the Cheeseboro RAWS, located 12 km from the fire. Live fuel moisture during the simulation was held constant at a value of 60-percent ODW for live herbaceous material and for live woody material.

Use of the most up-to-date map of fuels for the Santa Monica Mountains is inappropriate in a historical reconstruction because the current fuel type in the area of the 1996 Calabasas Fire reflects early postfire succession. Instead, a technique was devised to produce a fuels map to reflect the conditions in 1996, prior to the arrival of the fire. First, a map of the potential natural vegetation (PNV), the ultimate floristic composition an area would attain many years after fire, was generated (Franklin 1997). Second, the fire history of the Santa Monica Mountains was retabulated to reflect the age of each cell prior to the arrival of the Calabasas Fire. Finally, tables of successional pathways, referred to as regrowth files (.rgr), were used to cross reference each chaparral PNV type with age to yield a fuel type. The regrowth files included custom chaparral fuel models (Weise and Regelbrugge 1997) and were used to make maps showing custom fuels. Additionally, a custom fuel model for describing wildland-urban interface (WUI) was developed by combining the fuel loadings in the NFFL grass and southern rough fuel models.

Terrain elevation for the entire domain is available at 10 m spatial resolution. Since the spatial resolution of the fuels data is no better than 30 m, the elevation data were resampled from 10 to 30 m using bilinear interpolation prior to calculating slope and aspect at that resolution.

At 1-hour intervals during the course of the fire, a helicopter equipped with a global positioning system (GPS) receiver was used to map the location of the leading edge of the fire. These data serve as the historical record of fire spread to which the HFire and FARSITE simulations are referenced. The effects of suppression are unaccounted for in the simulations and therefore represent a potential source of error in comparing modeled and actual fire behavior. Suppression of the heading portion of the fire was largely unsuccessful during the first 4 hours of the fire, but suppression along the flanks of the fire during this time did have some effect.

Run Time Efficiency

Run time efficiency is an important attribute of a fire-spread model, both for the simulation of individual fires and simulations of long-term fire regimes. The run-time performance of HFire was evaluated relative to FARSITE for each of the historical fire simulations described in this paper. All of the simulations used in the timing analysis were performed on a personal computer with an Intel Core2 Duo dual-core processor, 2 gigabytes of RAM, and running the Windows XP 32-bit operating system.[5] Care was taken to ensure that the simulation was the only active task not associated with the operating system on the computer.

Results

Synthetic Landscape Tests

For all of the figures in this section, FARSITE perimeters are represented as black lines and HFire perimeters as colors representing regular intervals of fire progression. Sørensen metric values, quantitatively comparing HFire and FARSITE burned area at the final time step (S_f) for each model run, are included on the figures.

Test of different windspeeds—

The results of this test are presented in figures 1 and 2. As expected, as windspeed increases, the fires become larger, and the length-to-width ratio decreases (fig. 1). The one-dimensional, forward rate of spread is identical in all cases for HFire and FARSITE, the difference is in the flanking rate of spread and the resulting two-dimensional shape. FARSITE produces a rounded fire front, whereas HFire exhibits a triangular leading edge. Here, the increasingly sharp triangular edge corresponds to an increasingly stretched vertex of the eight-sided fire perimeter with increasing

---

[5] The use of trade or firm names in this publication is for user information and does not imply endorsement by the U.S. Department of Agriculture of any product or service.

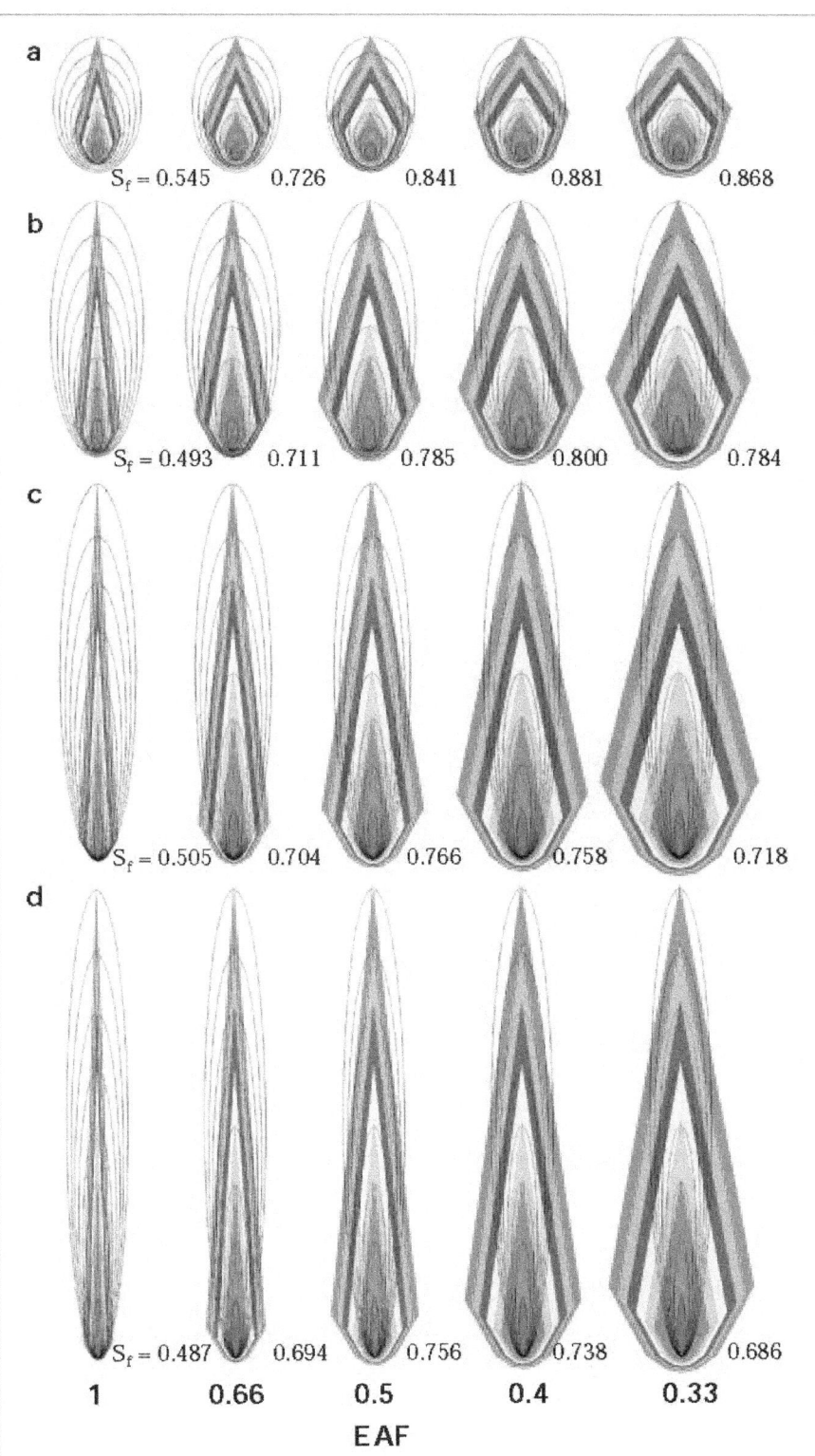

a

$S_f = 0.545$ 0.726   0.841   0.881   0.868

b

$S_f = 0.493$ 0.711   0.785   0.800   0.784

c

$S_f = 0.505$ 0.704   0.766   0.758   0.718

d

$S_f = 0.487$ 0.694   0.756   0.738   0.686

1   0.66   0.5   0.4   0.33

EAF

Figure 1—A test of varying windspeeds on flat terrain, showing HFire (colors) and FARSITE (lines) perimeters for (a) 5-m/s, (b) 10-m/s, (c) 15-m/s, and (d) 20-m/s winds; the length-to-width ratio of the ellipses increases as windspeed increases; HFire shown for ellipse adjustment factors (EAFs) (k in eqn. 2) of 1.0, 0.66, 0.5, 0.4, and 0.33.

windspeed. The back edge of the perimeter corresponds to the remaining six sides of the eight-sided figure, and has flat edges, although it appears rounded because they are close together.

To minimize the difference between HFire and FARSITE results, we ran HFire with five values of EAF. Setting EAF to 1.0 corresponds to no adjustment; values less than 1.0 decrease the length-to-width ratio, increasing the flanking rate of spread (eqn. 2). An EAF of 0.4 maximized the Sørensen metric between HFire and FARSITE at lower windspeeds. An EAF setting of 0.5 maximized the metric at higher windspeeds.

Figure 2 illustrates the special case of 0-m/s winds, in which the fire spreads in a circular pattern. Both HFire and FARSITE accurately capture the expected one-dimensional Rothermel rate of spread. For FARSITE, the modeled shape is a circle. The HFire algorithm approximates the circular shape with an octagon.

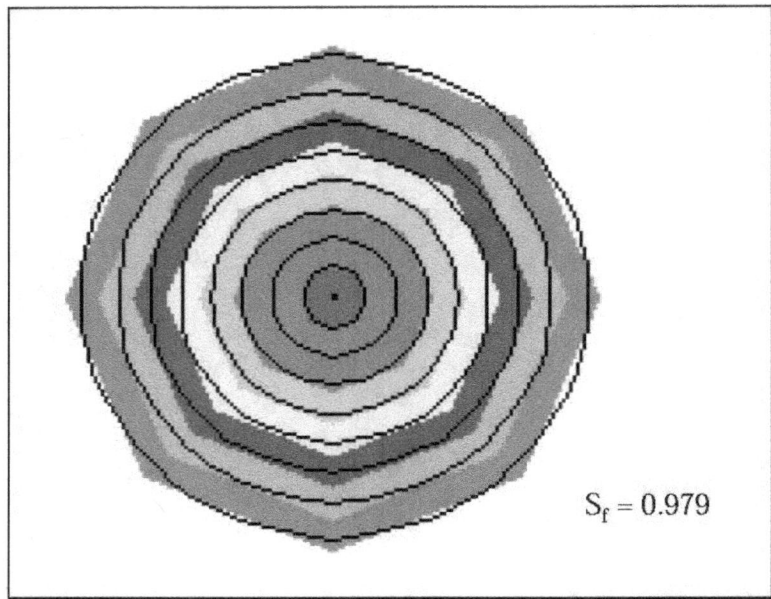

$$S_f = 0.979$$

Figure 2—Null windspeed test on flat terrain, showing HFire (colors) and FARSITE (lines) perimeters for 0 m/s winds; the fire is circular for FARSITE and octagonal for HFire.

Test of time varying wind direction —
Figure 3 shows that varying the wind inputs leads to HFire and FARSITE perimeters having closer agreement. Comparing the results of wind azimuth scenario 1 (fig. 3b) with those from the constant azimuth case (fig. 3a) shows that perturbing the wind direction slightly (a maximum of ±10 degrees) widens the fire front noticeably, eliciting better agreement with the FARSITE perimeters. Wind azimuth

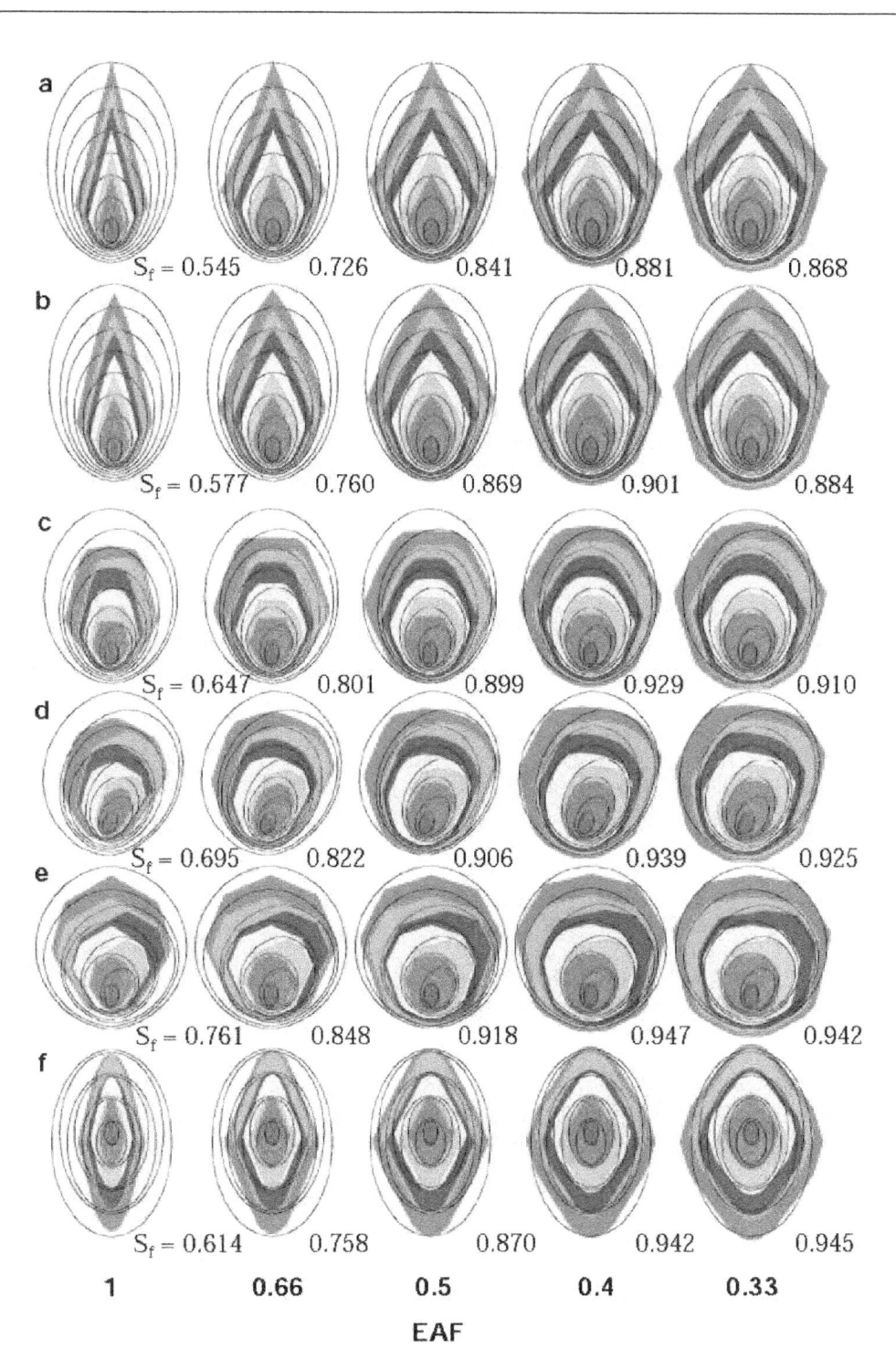

a

S_f = 0.545   0.726   0.841   0.881   0.868

b

S_f = 0.577   0.760   0.869   0.901   0.884

c

S_f = 0.647   0.801   0.899   0.929   0.910

d

S_f = 0.695   0.822   0.906   0.939   0.925

e

S_f = 0.761   0.848   0.918   0.947   0.942

f

S_f = 0.614   0.758   0.870   0.942   0.945

1   0.66   0.5   0.4   0.33

EAF

Figure 3 — A test of differing azimuth scenarios for 5-m/s winds, showing HFire (colors) and FARSITE (lines) perimeters for (a) constant azimuth, (b) azimuth scenario 1, (c) scenario 2, (d) scenario 3, (e) scenario 4, (f) scenario 5; there is better agreement between HFire- and FARSITE-modeled fire shapes as perturbations of the azimuth increase. HFire shown for ellipse adjustment factors (EAFs) of 1.0, 0.66, 0.5, 0.4, and 0.33.

scenarios 2 and 3, which perturb the wind direction a greater amount, resulted in a smooth, nontriangular fire front for HFire (fig. 3c and 3d). Hence, agreement between HFire and FARSITE improved, with Sørensen metric values above 0.9. Scenario 4 systematically perturbed the wind azimuth ±45 degrees about 180 degrees, leading to symmetric fire perimeters at the end of the simulation for both models, and a Sørensen metric value of 0.947 for an EAF of 0.4. Likewise, perturbing the wind ±180 degrees leads to symmetric shapes for both models, with a high Sørensen metric value of 0.942 (fig. 3f).

Test of different windspeeds and slopes, with up-slope winds —

Starting from the case of zero windspeed and zero slope, increasing windspeed has a greater effect on forward rate of spread than does increasing the slope by approximately a factor of two (fig. 4). Steepening the slope has a large effect on forward rate of spread at low windspeeds, but the effect at higher windspeeds is reduced. In all cases, forward rate of spread is comparable between HFire and FARSITE, with FARSITE exhibiting greater spread on the flanks of the fire.

Test of different slopes and cross-slope winds —

This test shows the largest difference between FARSITE and HFire perimeters as measured by the Sørensen metric. Differences arise because of the vector/eight nearest neighbor raster differences in the models. As the slope becomes steeper, the direction of fire propagation smoothly rotates from 90 degrees to approximately 60 degrees in the FARSITE simulations (fig. 5). HFire suffers from some distortion when the direction of fire spread is not aligned with one of the eight cardinal directions of the underlying lattice--the angles to the eight adjacent pixels. For the 0-, 20-, and 40-percent model runs, the true direction of fire propagation was approximately 90 degrees, so the HFire modeled perimeters are reasonable. For the 60- and 80-percent slope runs, HFire modeled the true direction of spread of approximately 75 degrees as a mixture of spread at 45 and 90 degrees. For the 100-percent slope, HFire modeled the true direction of spread (approximately 60 degrees) as propagating toward 45 degrees. Hence, agreement between modeled fire shapes is relatively poor (Sørensen metric values less than 0.8) for the 60-, 80-, and 100-percent slope comparisons. However, as demonstrated in the test of time varying wind direction, perturbing the wind azimuth (±20 degrees about 270 degrees) results in a more rounded fire front, leading to much closer agreement between the predicted fire shapes. The Sørensen metric values at the end of the simulation for the 60-, 80-, and 100-percent slope cases, where disagreement between FARSITE and HFire is highest, are 0.785, 0.718, and 0.669 for the constant 270 azimuth case but increase to 0.904, 0.909, and 0.848 for the 270 ± 20 azimuth case.

Increasing windspeed has a greater effect on forward rate of spread than does increasing the slope.

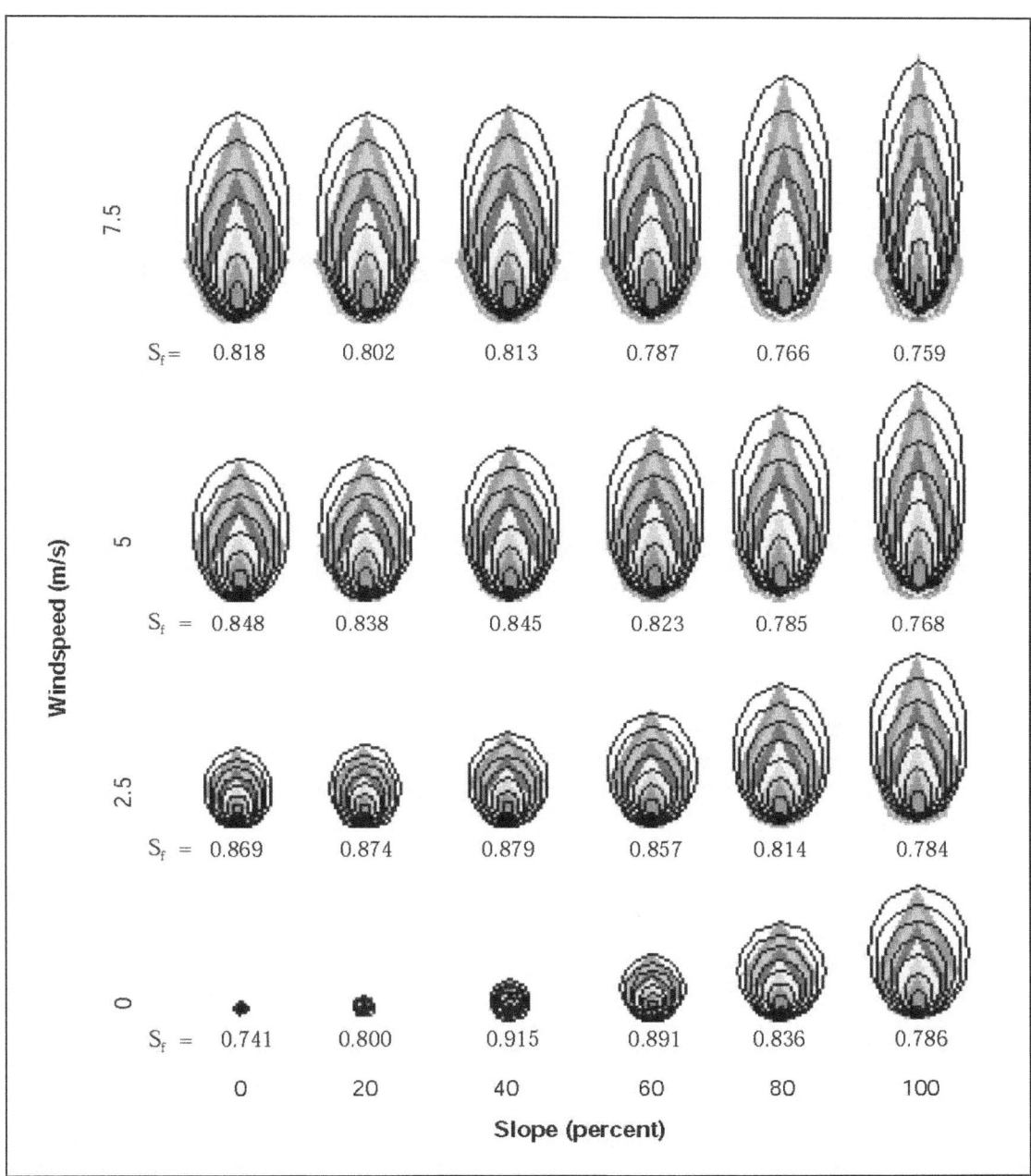

Figure 4—A test of differing windspeed and slope, with up-slope winds, showing HFire (colors) and FARSITE (lines) perimeters. The length-to-width ratio of the ellipses increases as windspeed and slope steepness increase.

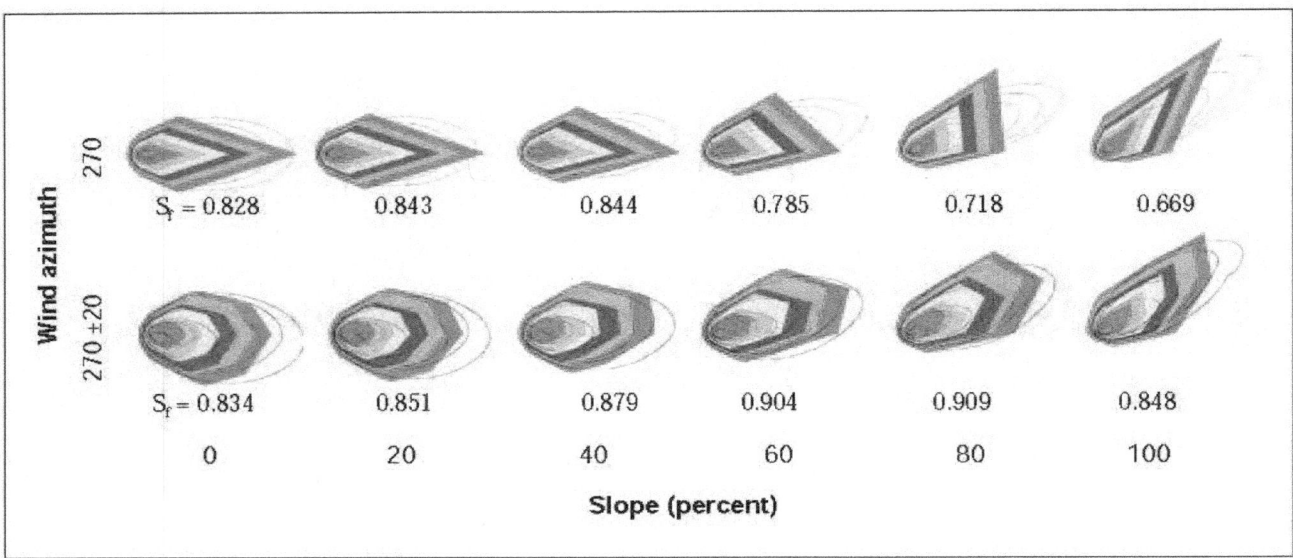

Figure 5—A test of 7.5-m/s windspeed, varying slope, and wind azimuth, with cross-slope winds, showing HFire (colors) and FARSITE (lines) perimeters. This test reveals raster-based limitations of HFire fire spread when the direction of spread is not in a cardinal direction; this effect is mitigated when wind azimuth is perturbed.

Test of different fuel model transitions—

The case involving homogeneous fuels exhibits the expected pattern of equivalent forward rate of spread, with FARSITE producing a wider fire front (fig. 6a). In the case involving the unburnable block, the fire perimeters for both models are unchanged, except for in the block (fig. 6b). The case with the slower burning block shows, once again, that more heterogeneous conditions lead to a closer match between HFire and FARSITE. For the EAF of 0.4 model run, the flanking fire spread for HFire on the left side of the fire (where two different fuels are encountered) is less than 1 hour behind FARSITE, whereas on the right flank, it is more than 1 hour behind (fig. 6c). The scenario where a faster burning block of fuel is encountered exhibited the strongest agreement. Unlike the cases involving the unburnable and slow-burning blocks, agreement in fire spread on both flanks of the fire improved upon encountering the different block of fuels, and final Sørensen metric values were greater than 0.9. Sørensen metric values were lower for the other three scenarios owning to the triangular fire front.

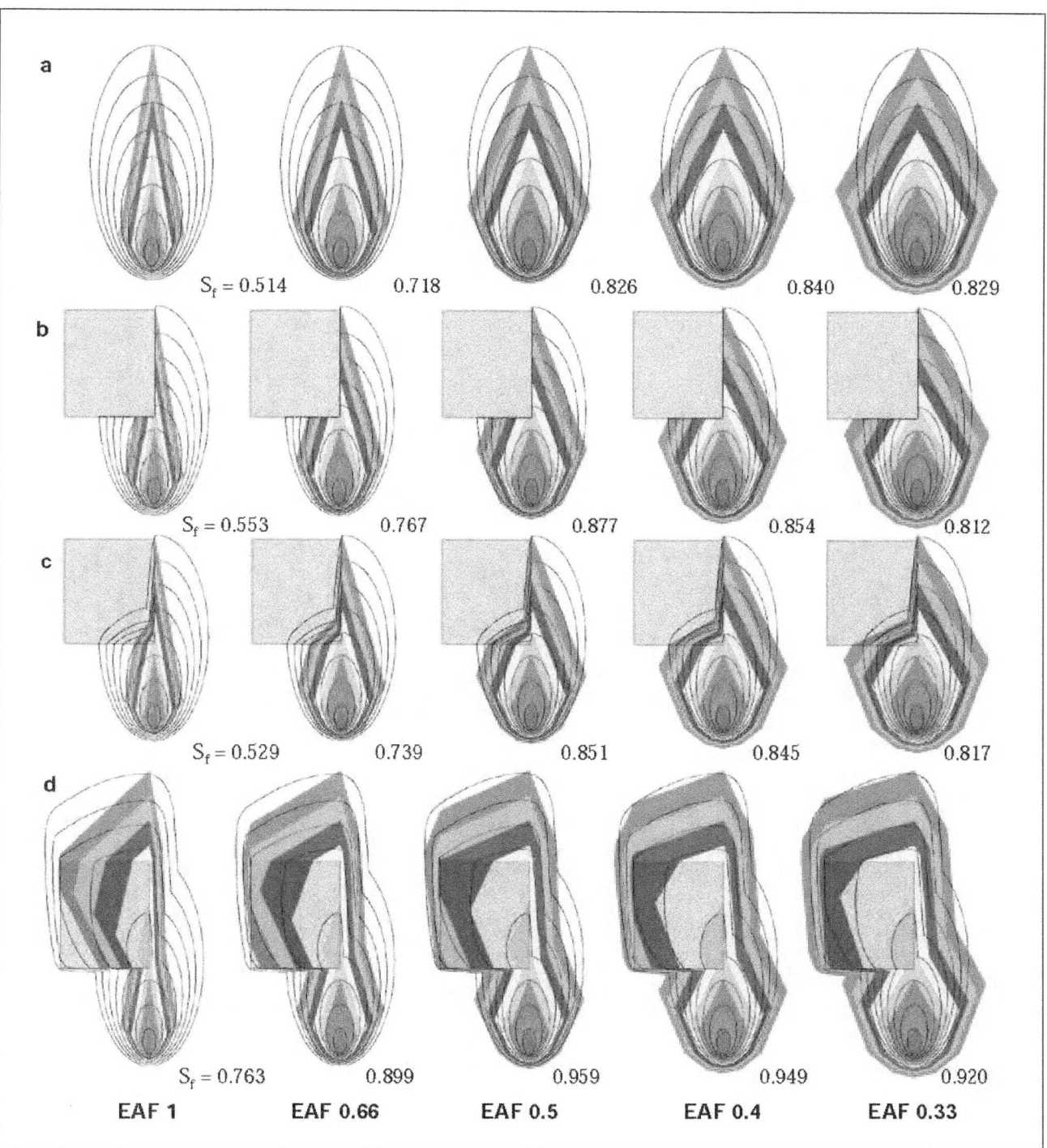

Figure 6—A test of different blocks of fuels with 7-m/s winds, showing HFire (colors) and FARSITE (lines) perimeters for four fuel model (FM) maps: (a) uniform FM 15, (b) FM 15 plus unburnable, (c) FM 15 plus slower burning, (d) FM 15 plus faster burning. Increased heterogeneity in fuels leads to better agreement between HFire- and FARSITE-modeled perimeters. HFire shown for ellipse adjustment factors (EAFs) of 1.0, 0.66, 0.5, 0.4, and 0.33.

Historical Fires

Day Fire results—

Figure 7 shows FARSITE and HFire (EAF of 0.5, 0.66, 0.9) perimeters for the Day Fire from 4 July 1500 hours to 6 July 2300 hours. The modeled fires were all roughly circular, with the EAF 0.5 fire being largest and the EAF 0.9 fire being smallest. The effect of altering EAF clearly has a greater effect on fire size than fire shape in heterogeneous conditions. Sørensen metric values between HFire- and FARSITE-modeled perimeters were highest for the EAF 0.66 model run, with values generally above 0.9 for the first 2 days of burning, and above 0.8 on the 3rd day. Complete Sørensen metric values are available in table 4.

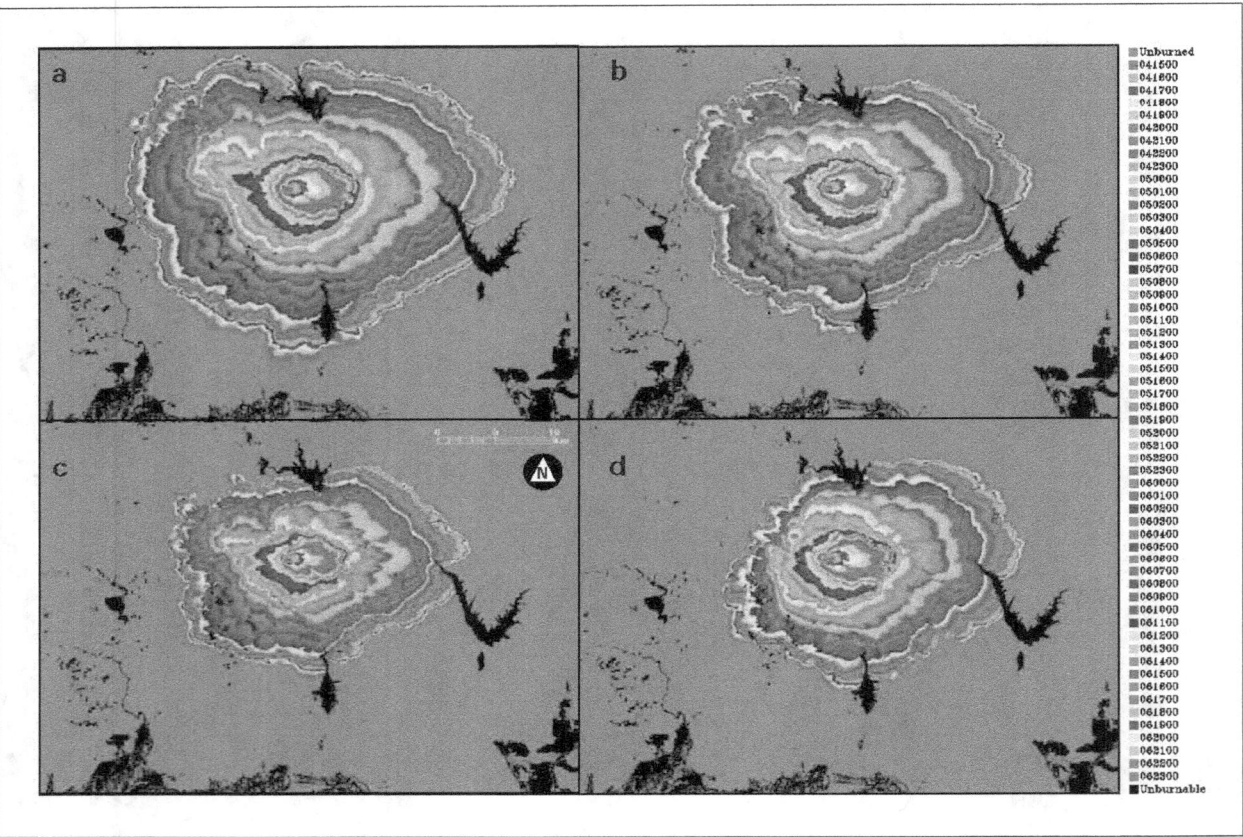

Figure 7—Simulated perimeters for the Day Fire; HFire shown for ellipse adjustment factors (EAFs) of (a) 0.5, (b) 0.66, (c) 0.9, and (d) FARSITE. The legend refers to fire perimeters at a given time, with time in DDHHMM format. Low windspeeds and a diurnal wind pattern lead to roughly circular fire shapes. HFire run with an EAF of 0.66 shows the best agreement with FARSITE perimeters; associated Sørensen metric scores are listed in table 4.

Table 4—Sørensen metric values for HFire (EAF set to 0.5, 0.66, and 0.9) and FARSITE for the Day Fire

EAF 0.5				EAF 0.66				EAF 0.9			
Time	Sørensen	Time	Sørensen	Time	Sørensen	Time	Sørensen	Time	Sørensen	Time	Sørensen
41500	0.819	51900	0.835	41500	0.774	51900	0.904	41500	0.632	51900	0.772
41600	0.922	52000	0.829	41600	0.919	52000	0.911	41600	0.827	52000	0.787
41700	0.898	52100	0.824	41700	0.899	52100	0.913	41700	0.792	52100	0.800
41800	0.875	52200	0.821	41800	0.877	52200	0.913	41800	0.725	52200	0.807
41900	0.889	52300	0.819	41900	0.907	52300	0.914	41900	0.729	52300	0.817
42000	0.902	60000	0.814	42000	0.915	60000	0.911	42000	0.732	60000	0.823
42100	0.918	60100	0.806	42100	0.94	60100	0.906	42100	0.777	60100	0.832
42200	0.92	60200	0.798	42200	0.959	60200	0.902	42200	0.813	60200	0.841
42300	0.914	60300	0.784	42300	0.965	60300	0.893	42300	0.833	60300	0.849
50000	0.905	60400	0.765	50000	0.966	60400	0.881	50000	0.853	60400	0.856
50100	0.898	60500	0.745	50100	0.962	60500	0.862	50100	0.861	60500	0.858
50200	0.89	60600	0.73	50200	0.96	60600	0.847	50200	0.859	60600	0.855
50300	0.878	60700	0.72	50300	0.962	60700	0.838	50300	0.853	60700	0.851
50400	0.876	60800	0.72	50400	0.958	60800	0.838	50400	0.849	60800	0.85
50500	0.876	60900	0.723	50500	0.959	60900	0.839	50500	0.859	60900	0.848
50600	0.864	61000	0.728	50600	0.957	61000	0.841	50600	0.869	61000	0.847
50700	0.857	61100	0.737	50700	0.957	61100	0.846	50700	0.868	61100	0.847
50800	0.855	61200	0.746	50800	0.96	61200	0.853	50800	0.865	61200	0.853
50900	0.847	61300	0.75	50900	0.949	61300	0.855	50900	0.859	61300	0.854
51000	0.838	61400	0.754	51000	0.937	61400	0.859	51000	0.855	61400	0.854
51100	0.835	61500	0.761	51100	0.925	61500	0.864	51100	0.832	61500	0.854
51200	0.839	61600	0.76	51200	0.911	61600	0.869	51200	0.809	61600	0.861
51300	0.846	61700	0.757	51300	0.904	61700	0.872	51300	0.789	61700	0.867
51400	0.85	61800	0.753	51400	0.898	61800	0.873	51400	0.779	61800	0.872
51500	0.845	61900	0.751	51500	0.899	61900	0.872	51500	0.779	61900	0.874
51600	0.843	62000	0.748	51600	0.894	62000	0.871	51600	0.776	62000	0.874
51700	0.839	62100	0.745	51700	0.89	62100	0.87	51700	0.767	62100	0.875
51800	0.84	62200	0.742	51800	0.892	62200	0.869	51800	0.763	62200	0.875
—	—	62300	0.739	—	—	62300	0.868	—	—	62300	0.875

The EAF 0.66 model run shows the highest agreement with FARSITE, with Sørensen values on the order of 0.9.
Time in DHHHH format.
EAF = ellipse adjustment factor.

These simulations of the Day Fire demonstrate that HFire and FARSITE produce similar fire perimeters under low wind conditions. Low wind conditions during the early portion of the fire were amenable to successful fire suppression efforts, and the fire was actively suppressed. Because of the suppression, modeled HFire and FARSITE perimeters are approximately five times the size of a MODIS active fire product-derived reference perimeter for the same time step (fig. 8).

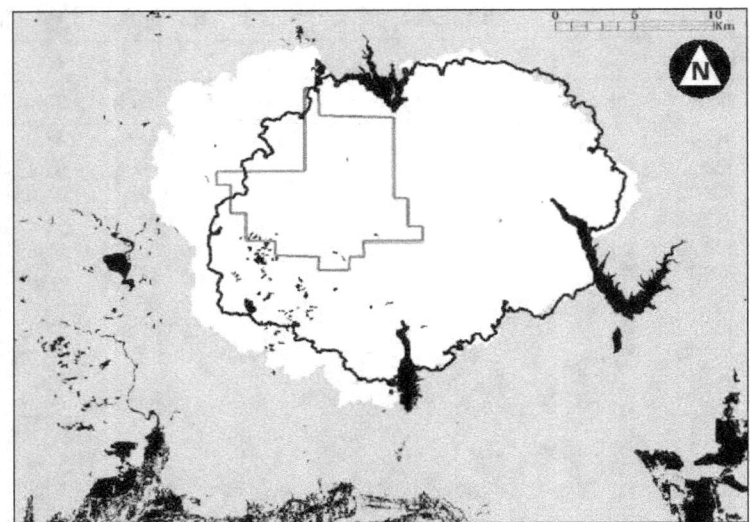

Figure 8—Day Fire perimeters at 2300 hours on 6 September: Hfire (white), FARSITE (black), MODIS (red). The green color represents available fuels, and the black color represents unburnable areas. The discrepancy in fire size between the modeled fires and the actual fire is attributable to fire suppression.

Simi Fire results—

Figure 9 shows HFire and FARSITE perimeters for the Simi Fire from 1400 hours on 25 October to 2300 hours on 26 October. HFire is shown for an EAF of 0.66, which provided the highest overall agreement. The shapes of initial fire progression to the southwest are very similar, with forward rate of spread slightly faster for FARSITE. The flanking rate of spread was slightly faster for HFire. The HFire simulation reached the western edge of Simi Valley ("b" on fig. 9) at 0900 hours on 26 October, whereas the FARSITE simulation reaches the same landmark at 1200 hours. Other features of note include the expansion of HFire perimeters into areas that FARSITE did not burn, to the north and to the west (marked a and b on fig. 9). HFire was better able to utilize narrow corridors to reach additional areas of fuel. FARSITE was run with a perimeter resolution of 99 m. A finer resolution may have allowed FARSITE to navigate these corridors; however, finer resolution results in very long model run times for FARSITE (on the order of 3 to 7 days) and the finest resolution that the model was successfully run at in prior research for the Simi Fire was 59 m (Peterson et al. 2005). This is twice the resolution at which HFire was run, 30 m, which is the native resolution of the landscape variables. Fire spread in the south-central portion of the fire (marked c on fig. 8) further illustrates this point. Both HFire and FARSITE show fire just north of point c at 1700 hours on 25 October. HFire propagated fire to the southwest during the next hour, whereas FARSITE required 5 hours to get through the corridor. This has implications for

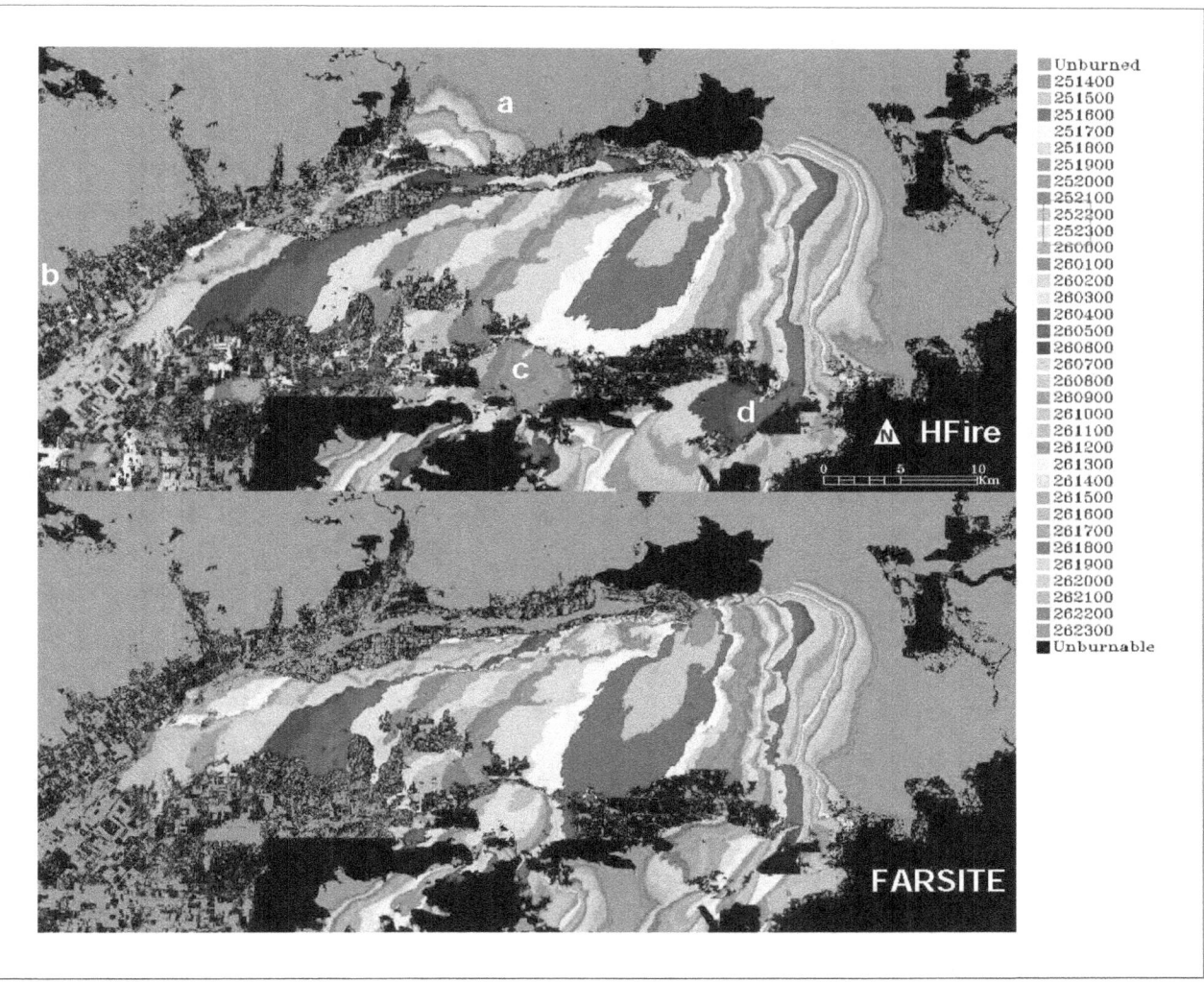

Figure 9—Simulated perimeters for the Simi Fire for HFire (EAF 0.66) and FARSITE. The legend refers to fire perimeters at a given time, with time in DDHHMM format. Sørensen metric scores are listed in table 5. FARSITE propagates the fire slightly faster in the forward-spread direction, whereas HFire is faster in the flanking direction; additionally, HFire is better able to navigate narrow fuel corridors, fire spread at point a and b is only present in the HFire perimeters, and fire spread at c and d occurs earlier in the HFire simulations.

fires in the WUI where narrow corridors may be common. Despite these areas of disagreement, Sørensen metric values were again high, generally on the order of 0.85 to 0.9, because of the large area in the main body of the fire, which overlaps for the two models. Complete Sørensen metric values are available in table 5.

Figure 10 shows perimeters derived from HFire, FARSITE, and MODIS: 2300 hours on 25 October for the models and 2233 hours on 25 October for MODIS, and 1200 hours on 26 October for the models and 1209 hours on 26 October for MODIS. For the first comparison, the HFire and FARSITE perimeters were nearly

Table 5—Sørensen metric values for HFire (EAF[a] set to 0.66) and FARSITE for the Simi Fire[b]

Time[c]	Sørensen	Time	Sørensen
251400	0.714	260700	0.854
251500	0.769	260800	0.852
251600	0.827	260900	0.845
251700	0.926	261000	0.847
251800	0.944	261100	0.84
251900	0.924	261200	0.838
252000	0.905	261300	0.837
252100	0.898	261400	0.842
252200	0.901	261500	0.846
252300	0.915	261600	0.851
260000	0.915	261700	0.856
260100	0.915	261800	0.859
260200	0.917	261900	0.862
260300	0.904	262000	0.864
260400	0.899	262100	0.865
260500	0.888	262200	0.865
260600	0.860	262300	0.866

[a] EAF = ellipse adjustment factor.
[b] Accuracy is lower at the beginning and end of the model runs, at the beginning FARSITE is propagating the fire more quickly, at the end the HFIRE modeled fire is larger as it is better able to negotiate narrow fuel isthmuses.
[c] Time in DDHHHH format.

identical on the east and west flanks of the fire. However, HFire exhibited greater spread to the southwest. Both modeled perimeters agreed well with MODIS (Sørensen metric values on the order of 0.75). The value for HFire was slightly lower because of overburning to the southwest. Fire suppression during the Simi Fire is only anecdotally documented, but as mentioned in the previous paragraph, the area of overburning by HFIRE at point c is separated from the main body of the landscape by a narrow corridor, so fire suppression efforts could have been focused on the small area, enhancing success. Additionally, MODIS resolution is coarse at 1 km, so the precision of the MODIS shape is uncertain.

For the second comparison, the modeled fires and the actual fire have reached the farthest western extent of the Simi Fire. HFire overburned farther to the west, whereas FARSITE was not able to negotiate the narrow fuel corridors to the west. Both modeled fires also overburn to the south and the southeast. This overburning of modeled fires relative to the MODIS perimeter likely reflects the presence of active fire suppression. Again, anecdotal information suggests that fire suppression was active to the south owing to the presence of the Ronald Reagan Presidential Library and other areas of high-value real estate. Sørensen metric values are lower for this comparison, owing to overburning.

Calabasas Fire results —

Figure 11 shows the fire perimeters for HFire (EAF 0.66) and FARSITE for the single-ignition case, with the fire igniting at 1100 hours and burning until 2200 hours. As for the Day and Simi Fires, agreement was highest for the 0.66 EAF case, and only EAF of 0.66 results are presented. The FARSITE simulation reaches the southern boundary approximately 1 hour sooner than HFire, but, in general, the shape and size of the fires are very similar. Sørensen metric values were on the order of 0.8 to 0.9.

However, comparing figures 11 and 12 reveals that agreement between the actual perimeters (fig. 12) and perimeters from both models (fig. 11) is poor. This is likely due to effective fire suppression efforts. The actual fire was much narrower during the initial 1100- to 1500-hours burning period, and was nearly controlled, before it spotted over Malibu Canyon road, igniting the second stage of the fire. Because of the compounding errors owing to not accounting for fire suppression, HFire and FARSITE were rerun, treating the northern and southern halves of the fire separately.

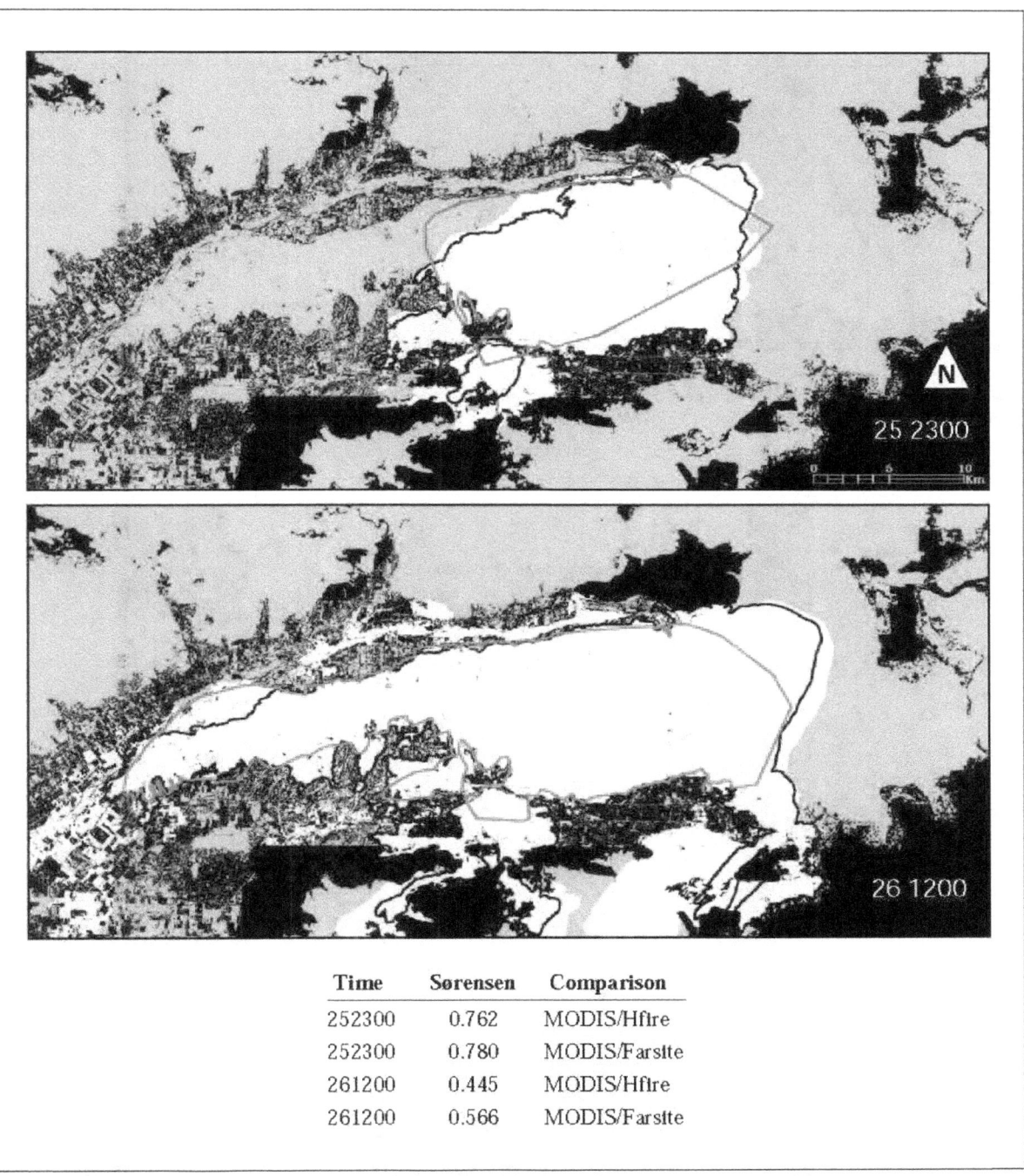

Time	Sørensen	Comparison
252300	0.762	MODIS/Hfire
252300	0.780	MODIS/Farsite
261200	0.445	MODIS/Hfire
261200	0.566	MODIS/Farsite

Figure 10—Simi Fire perimeters: HFire (white), FARSITE (black), and MODIS reference (red), for 2 hours of the Simi Fire, 2300 hours 25 October and 1200 hours 26 October. Times are in DDHHMM format. The green color represents available fuels, and the black color represents unburnable areas. Agreement is good for the first comparison; agreement for the second comparison is hindered because the actual fire was actively suppressed.

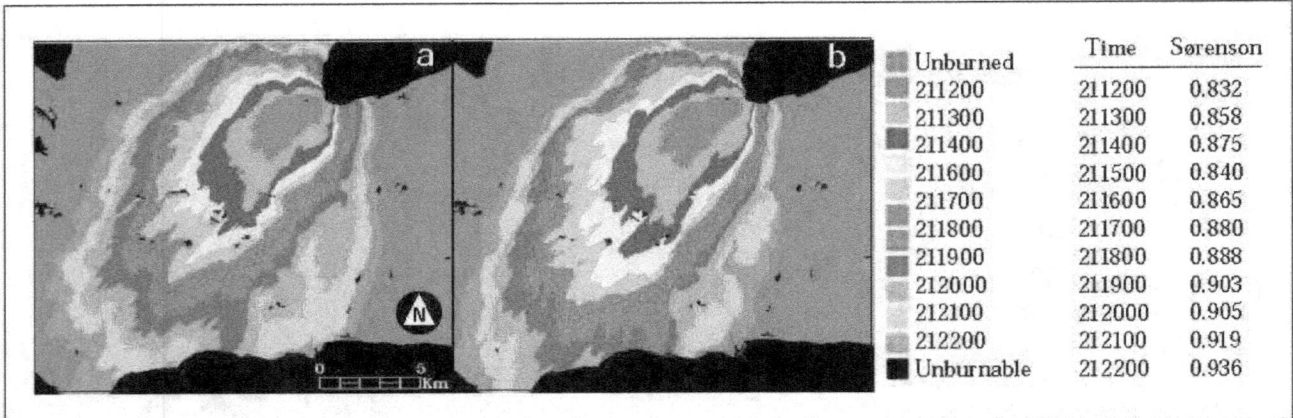

Figure 11—Simulated perimeters for the Calabasas Fire for (a) HFire (EAF 0.66) and (b) FARSITE. The legend refers to fire perimeters at a given time, with time in DDHHMM format. Sørensen metric scores are included. Agreement is high throughout the simulation period.

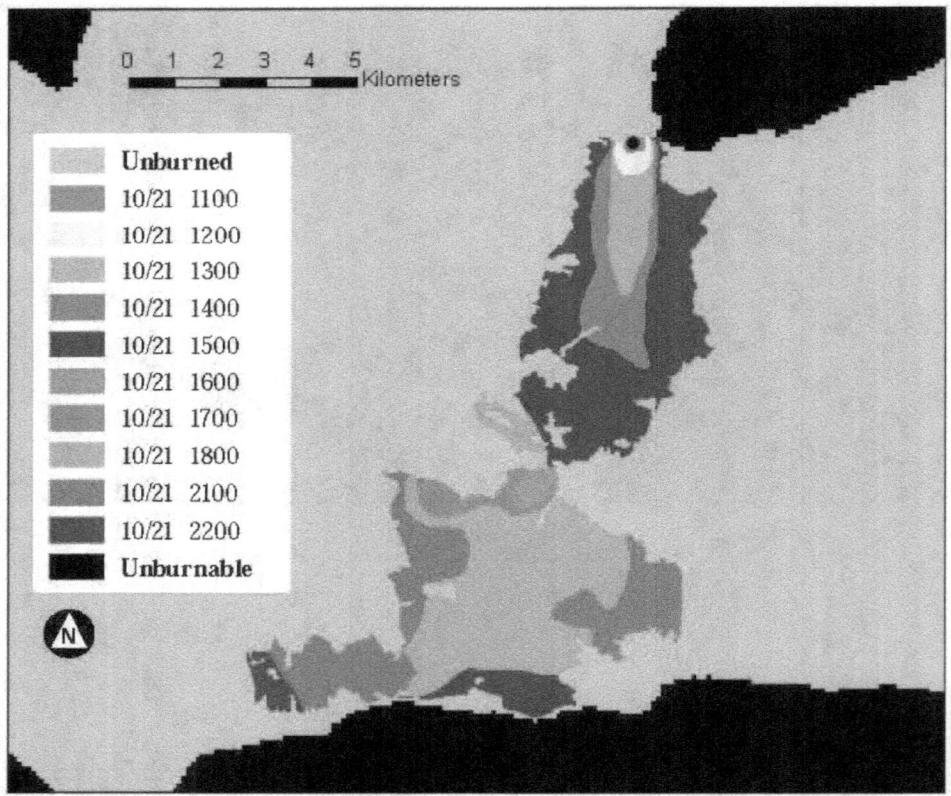

Figure 12 — Fire perimeters for the Calabasas Fire determined by helicopter reconnaissance. The pinched shape at 1500 hours is due to successful fire suppression efforts, which were nearly successful until the fire spotted over containment lines between 1500 and 1600 hours. The legend refers to fire perimeters at a given time, with time in MonthMonth/DD HHMM format.

Figure 13 shows HFire, FARSITE, and actual perimeters at two times following the initial ignition at 1100 hours and two times following the spot fire ignition at 1500 hours. At 1300 and 1500 hours, both the azimuth and size of the modeled and actual fires differ. In contrast, modeled fire perimeters at the two later times, associated with the spot fire ignition, exhibit better agreement with the actual fire in both direction and magnitude of fire spread. Both the actual and modeled fires reached the southern end of the landscape (the Pacific Ocean) within the same hour. The modeled fires are narrower than the actual fire at 1800 hours but are on the same order of magnitude at 2200 hours. Sørensen metric values between HFire and the actual fire are also much higher at 1800 and 2200 hours than at 1300 and 1500 hours, on the order of 0.7 vs. 0.2.

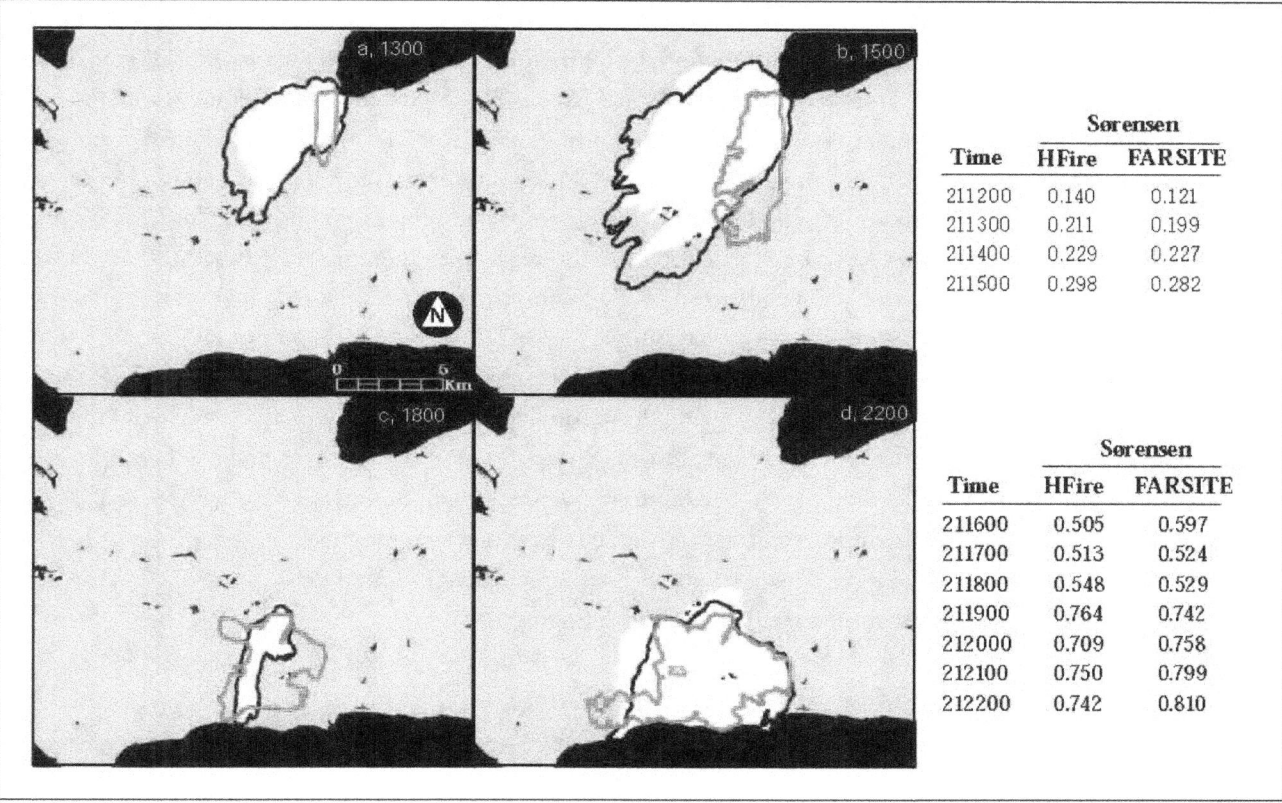

| | Sørensen | |
Time	HFire	FARSITE
211200	0.140	0.121
211300	0.211	0.199
211400	0.229	0.227
211500	0.298	0.282

| | Sørensen | |
Time	HFire	FARSITE
211600	0.505	0.597
211700	0.513	0.524
211800	0.548	0.529
211900	0.764	0.742
212000	0.709	0.758
212100	0.750	0.799
212200	0.742	0.810

Figure 13—Calabasas Fire perimeters: HFire (white), FARSITE (black), and helicopter reference (red), for the initial ignition and the spot fire ignition. The green color represents available fuels, and the black color represents unburnable areas. The 1300- and 1500-hour perimeters result from the initial ignition at 1200 hours; the 1800- and 2200-hour perimeters result from the spot fire ignition at 1500 hours, times are in DDHHMM format. Sørensen metric scores are included. The first set of simulations show poor agreement with reality because the wind azimuth recorded at the Cheeseboro remote automated weather station (RAWS) was not representative of the winds affecting the fire; agreement was better during the second simulation period.

Run Time Efficiency

The wall clock times required for the simulation of 58 hours of the Day Fire, 35 hours of the Simi Fire, and 12 hours of the Calabasas Fire were recorded. All FARSITE simulations were performed with perimeter and distance resolution set to 99 m. Resolution values closer to the native resolution (30 m) of the input terrain and fuels significantly increase the run time without a substantial increase in accuracy (Peterson et al. 2005). FARSITE took 2.3 times as long as HFire (6.33 min) to complete the simulation of the Day Fire (14.83 min). The relatively small difference can be attributed to the relatively homogeneous landscape and low wind conditions used as inputs to these simulations. The Calabasas Fire was more complex, involving varying terrain and fuels and higher windspeeds. HFire (1.1 min) completed the simulation in approximately one-eighth the time for FARSITE (8.75 min). The Simi Fire was the most complex simulation, covering the largest area. HFire (6.1 min) completed the simulation approximately 162 times faster than FARSITE (16.5 h).

Figure 14 illustrates model run times for each hour of the Simi Fire with cumulative area burned (x-axis) plotted versus HFire and FARSITE run times on separate y-axes. The trend for HFire is approximately linear, which implies that the run time is proportional to the number of ignited cells. The trend for FARSITE is more complex. It is approximately linear from the time of ignition until 30 000 ha burned, which occurred at 200 hours on 26 October. During this initial period, the fire shape was relatively simple (fig. 9). The period from 400 to 1300 hours on 26 October exhibits the steepest slope (longest model run time in comparison to the net area burned). During this period, the perimeter length and complexity increased relative to the area burned as the fire expanded to the south and southeast (points c and d on fig. 9). The increased perimeter length leads to longer calculation times because more vertices are added to the perimeter to meet the specified perimeter resolution. The inset on the main graph of figure 14, a log-log plot of run time vs. area burned, emphasizes these findings.

Discussion

Predictions from HFire were similar to those obtained from FARSITE for a standard set of benchmarks developed by Finney (1998) for the testing of the FARSITE model. Although the predictions from HFire and FARSITE for the benchmarks are virtually identical in the direction of the maximum rate of fire spread, there are differences between the models in their predicted shapes, and hence for fire spread along the flanks. Similar shapes are shown in French et al. (1990) and Ball and Guertin (1992), and are inherent to eight-nearest-neighbors raster fire-spread

Run time is proportional to the number of ignited cells.

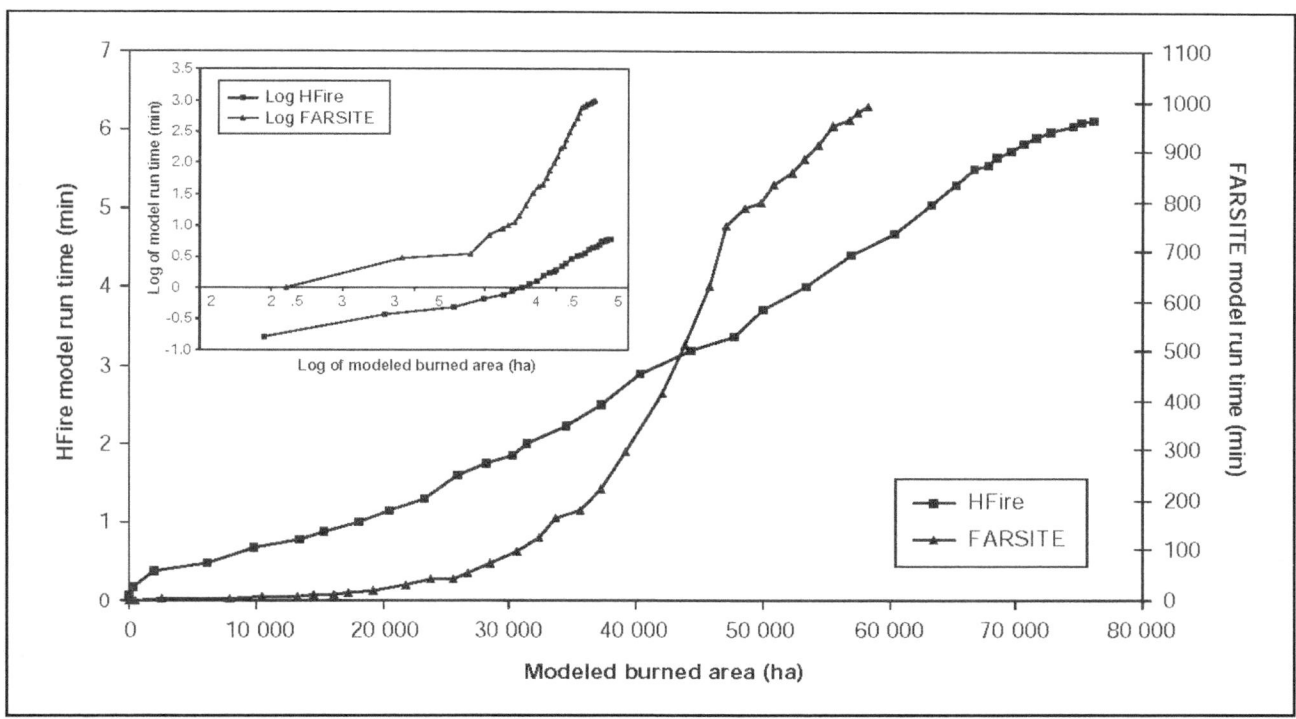

Figure 14—Model run times for the Simi Fire for HFire and FARSITE, on separate axes. HFire shows a consistent relationship between fire size and model run time throughout the 6-minute burn time. The model run time is 16.5 hours for FARSITE, with run time for a particular hourly time step being dependent on the fire shape. Inset is a log-log plot of run time with HFire and FARSITE run times on the same axis to emphasize differences.

models. There are raster models that better approximate an elliptical fire shape, such as FlamMap (Finney 2006) and the Finney minimum travel time model (Finney 2002). However, although both models allow for a heterogeneous landscape, weather conditions are held constant. The constant weather simplifies the fire-spread calculations, so a large neighborhood of pixels can be used to populate the available angles in equation (3) (as opposed to multiples of 45 degrees), and an elliptical shape is better realized. Owing to the constant weather requirement, neither model is used to simulate actual fires.

The differences in shape were reduced for the more complex benchmark tests, which are closer to conditions that could occur during an actual fire. In figure 3, Sørensen metric values are higher for the more varying wind scenarios (d, e, and f). In figure 5, varying the wind azimuth by ±20 degrees increased agreement between FARSITE- and HFire-modeled shapes dramatically for the steeper slope scenarios. In figure 6, it can be seen the models respond similarly to transitions to different fuel types.

Similarly, the pointed shape that is observed in some of the predictions from HFire for the benchmarks on homogeneous landscapes is not apparent in the simulations of historical fires. For instance, both FARSITE and HFire modeled the Day Fire as having a generally circular shape, owing to low windspeeds and alternating wind directions during the simulation period (fig. 7). Lower windspeeds favor more circular fires (fig. 1 and 2) and from 1400 hours on 4 September to 2300 hours on 6 September, windspeeds were greater than 5 m/s only 7 of 58 hours, the maximum windspeed was 6.7 m/s, and the median windspeed was 3.1 m/s. Additionally, because the wind alternates in a typical diurnal pattern between easterly in the mornings and westerly in the afternoons, wind did not have a net directional effect on fire spread. This is similar to the time varying wind direction test, where alternating wind conditions in Wind Azimuth Scenario 5 lead to an oval fire shape.

HFire and FARSITE produced generally similar fire perimeters in simulations of the Simi Fire, although HFire is better able to negotiate narrow fuel corridors in the terrain, which led to extended fire perimeters to the north and west, and earlier expansion to the south. The general location of the modeled fire fronts with respect to the reference data was good, although the fire-spread models, which do not include information about fire suppression, tend to overpredict areas of fire spread. Additionally, for the Simi and Day Fires, there is a disconnect between the spatial resolution of the model (30 m) and MODIS reference data (1 km). Figure 10 shows that the MODIS-based perimeters are more angular. However, the differences between modeled and reference perimeters involve large areas, not subtle differences at the edges owing to resolution, so resolution is less of an issue.

Correspondence between modeled and actual fire perimeters is affected by active fire suppression.

Simulations of the Calabasas Fire again demonstrate that HFire and FARSITE produce similar fire perimeters, and that correspondence between modeled and actual fire perimeters is affected by active fire suppression. Additionally, the wind data appear to have an effect on accuracy with respect to the reference perimeters, as the modeled direction of fire spread differed from the actual direction. The Cheeseboro RAWS is located 6 km northwest of the initial ignition point of the fire. Wind data from the Malibu RAWS, which is located 10 km south-southeast of the initial ignition point, were also examined but contained periods of winds blowing from the south, so predictions showed less agreement with the historical perimeters. The Santa Monica Mountains have complex topography, so it is plausible that the winds are subject to topographic steering, and only a RAWS within the same canyon as a fire would provide accurate wind azimuth data. An alternate explanation is that as RAWS "hourly" wind data are not actually hourly averages, but rather the average of the wind conditions 5 minutes prior to the reading, the data could be biased.

It is important to note that the 0.66 EAF model run led to the best agreement between HFire and FARSITE for all three historical fires. This differs from the synthetic landscape cases where EAF values of 0.4 and 0.5 were best (an EAF value closer to zero was needed to widen the fire shape in the homogeneous cases). The tests of time varying wind azimuth and different fuel model transitions demonstrated that HFire shows better agreement with FARSITE under shifting conditions. In actual fire conditions, where landscape and wind are varying simultaneously, the combined effect is to reduce the need for the EAF (a value closer to 1.0 is used).

The tests on synthetic landscapes and historical fires demonstrate that the raster and vector implementations of the Rothermel equation perform similarly. Further, the agreement between HFire and FARSITE perimeters for all three historical fires is qualitatively comparable to the agreement shown between the raster and vector implementations of the Canadian fire-spread model in figures 13 and 14 of Yassemi et al. (2008). However, there were some systematic discrepancies when comparisons were made to reference perimeters. Finney (1998) noted three main problems when simulating actual fires: (1) the model input data (both fuels and weather) may contain errors, (2) the resolution (both spatial and temporal) of the input data is not fine enough to account for natural variability, and (3) validation is hindered by errors associated with the reference perimeters. To this list we would add the difficulty in acquiring fire suppression information and incorporating it into models. Nevertheless, comparisons for the Simi Fire and the spot fire of the Calabasas Fire show that fire-spread models do have the potential to accurately predict fire-spread rates.

Similar to other raster models, the performance of HFire is proportional to the number of ignited cells and the rate of spread of the fastest burning cell. In contrast, FARSITE model performance is a function of the user-specified simulation resolution, the heterogeneity of the conditions through which the fire is burning (highly heterogeneous conditions increase the number of sub-time steps in a time step), and the amount and complexity of the fire perimeter crossovers, mergers, and islands to be resolved during the fire perimeter generation process. The effect of amount of crossovers to resolve can be seen for the Simi Fire. Differences in run time between HFire and FARSITE for the Simi Fire at the fourth time step are of the same order of magnitude as for the Calabasas Fire: HFire burned 10 000 ha in less than 1 minute, FARSITE in just under 10 minutes. The difference in run time between HFire and FARSITE for the Simi Fire became accentuated as the fire grew larger (fig. 14).

The tests on synthetic landscapes and historical fires demonstrate that the raster and vector implementations of the Rothermel equation perform similarly.

Conclusions

To evaluate performance and improve understanding of optimal parameterization, we compared HFire to FARSITE over a series of synthetic landscapes with varying conditions and for three historical fires. In the synthetic landscape comparisons, HFire showed good agreement with FARSITE in the heading direction. Additionally, HFire- and FARSITE-predicted fire shapes showed good agreement when burning conditions were more complex. The two models also performed similarly in the historical fires tests, with Sørensen metric values at the final timestep of 0.868, 0.866, and 0.936 for the Day, Simi, and Calabasas Fires, respectively.

HFire represents an attractive alternative to FARSITE because it provides a similar level of accuracy with orders of magnitude improvement in computation time, and very similar input data requirements. The increased algorithmic efficiency makes possible near real-time estimates of fire spread, such as might be available in a mobile or other embedded device that can be worn by firefighters on the fire line. It also provides a vehicle for quantitative estimate of fire risk for a locale through testing hundreds of different fuel treatment, fuel moisture, and fire suppression scenarios under different weather conditions (e.g., Finney 2001). Finally, HFire is ideal for mechanistic simulation of long-term fire regimes under different climate change and WUI expansion scenarios, enhancing our ability to understand underlying controls on fire patterns and to mitigate the effect of anthropogenic changes.

The comparisons between modeled and actual fire perimeters demonstrate the utility of fire models as a tool for wildland management, policy and hazard estimation. Future enhancements of HFire may include (1) modification of the fire-spread equation and rules (if Rothermel is updated or replaced), (2) addition of a spotting module, (3) addition of a suppression module that allows for scenario testing, (4) addition of a module for assessing the worth of fuel treatments.

The 2003 and 2007 southern California Wildfires have raised public awareness of the impact of wildfires on urban communities and increased concerns about potential future fire hazards associated with climate change. Given how little we know about climate change impacts on fire probabilities (Moritz and Stephens, in press) and the importance of fire-spread models as the basis of simulating ecological disturbance regimes, new and more physically based approaches are needed. The computational efficiency of the HFire algorithm creates opportunities for mechanistic fire models to play quantitative and dynamic roles in analysis of fire patterns.

The computational efficiency of the HFire algorithm creates opportunities for mechanistic fire models to play quantitative and dynamic roles in analysis of fire patterns.

Acknowledgments

This work was supported by the James S. McDonnell Foundation, the David and Lucile Packard Foundation, National Science Foundation Grant DMR-0606092, the Institute for Collaborative Biotechnologies through Army Research Office grant DAAD19-03-D-0004, and a National Aeronautics and Space Administration Regional Earth Science Application Center grant (CSDH NASA RESAC 447633-59075).

English Equivalents

When you know:	Multiply by:	To find:
Centimeters (cm)	0.394	Inches
Meters (m)	3.28	Feet
Kilometers (km)	0.621	Miles
Square meters (m^2)	10.76	Square feet
Hectares (ha)	2.47	Acres
Cubic meters (m^3)	35.3	Cubic feet
Meters per second (m/s)	2.24	Miles per hour
Joules (J)	0.000952	British thermal units
Kilograms (kg)	2.205	Pounds
Kilograms per cubic meter (kg/m^3)	0.0624	Pounds per cubic foot
Megagrams per hectare (Mg/ha)	0.446	Tons per acre

References

Albini, F.A. 1976. Estimating wildfire behavior and effects. Gen. Tech. Rep. INT-GTR-30. Ogden, UT: U.S. Department of Agriculture, Forest Service, Intermountain Forest and Range Experiment Station. 92 p.

Albini, F.A.; Baughman, R.G. 1979. Estimating windspeeds for predicting wildland fire behavior. Res. Pap. INT-RP-221. Ogden, UT: U.S. Department of Agriculture, Forest Service, Intermountain Forest and Range Experiment Station. 12 p.

Albini, F.A.; Chase, C.H. 1980. Fire containment equations for pocket calculators. Res. Pap. INT-RP-268. Ogden, UT: U.S. Department of Agriculture, Forest Service, Intermountain Forest and Range Experiment Station. 17 p.

Anderson, D.G.; Catchpole, E.A.; DeMestre, N.J.; Parkes, E. 1982. Modeling the spread of grass fires. Journal of the Australian Mathematical Society: Series B–Applied Mathematics. 23: 451–466.

Anderson, H.E. 1983. Predicting wind-driven wildland fire size and shape. Res. Pap. INT-RP-305. Ogden, UT: U.S. Department of Agriculture, Forest Service, Intermountain Forest and Range Experiment Station. 26 p.

Anderson, K.; Reuter, G.; Flannigan, M.D. 2007. Fire-growth modelling using meteorological data with random and systematic perturbations. International Journal of Wildland Fire. 16: 174–182.

Andrews, P.L. 1986. BEHAVE: Fire Behavior Prediction and Fuel Modeling Subsystem- BURN Subsystem, Part 1. Gen. Tech. Rep. INT-GTR-194. Ogden, UT: U.S. Department of Agriculture, Forest Service, Intermountain Forest and Range Experiment Station. 130 p.

Ball, G.L.; Guertin, D.P. 1992. Improved fire growth modeling. International Journal of Wildland Fire. 2: 47–54.

Beer, T. 1990. The Interaction of Wind and Fire. Boundary-Layer Meteorology. 54: 287–308.

Berjak, S.G.; Hearne, J.W. 2002. An improved cellular automaton model for simulating fire in a spatially heterogeneous Savanna system. Ecological Modeling. 148: 133–151.

Burgan, R.E.; Rothermel, R.C. 1984. BEHAVE: Fire Behavior Prediction and Fuel Modeling System—FUEL Subsystem. Gen. Tech. Rep. INT-GTR-167. Ogden, UT: U.S. Department of Agriculture, Forest Service, Intermountain Forest and Range Experiment Station. 126 p.

Butler, B.W.; Finney, M.; Bradshaw, L.; Forthofer, J.; McHugh, C.; Stratton, R.; Jimenez, D. 2006. WindWizard: a new tool for fire management decision support. In: Andrews, P.L.; Butler, B.W., eds. Proceedings, Fuels management— how to measure success conference. Proc. RMRS-P-41. Fort Collins, CO: U.S. Department of Agriculture, Forest Service, Rocky Mountain Research Station: 787–796.

Catchpole, T.; DeMestre, N. 1986. Physical models for a spreading line fire. Australian Forestry. 49: 102–111.

Clark, R.E.; Hope, A.S.; Tarantola, S.; Gatelli, D.; Dennison, P.E.; Moritz, M.A. [In press]. Sensitivity analysis of a fire spread model in a chaparral landscape. Fire Ecology.

Clarke, K.C.; Brass, J.A.; Riggan, P.J. 1994. A cellular automaton model of wildfire propagation and extinction. Photogrammetric Engineering and Remote Sensing. 60: 1355–1367.

Coleman, J.R.; Sullivan, A.L. 1996. A real-time computer application for the prediction of fire spread across the Australian landscape. Simulation. 67: 230–240.

Countryman, C.M.; Dean, W.H. 1979. Measuring moisture content in living chaparral: a field user's manual. Gen. Tech. Rep. PSW-GTR-36. Berkeley, CA: U.S. Department of Agriculture, Forest Service, Pacific Southwest Forest and Range Experiment Station. 27 p.

Dennison, P.E.; Roberts, D.A.; Peterson, S.H.; Rechel, J. 2005. Use of normalized difference water index for monitoring live fuel moisture. International Journal of Remote Sensing. 26: 1035–1042.

Dennison, P.E.; Roberts, D.A.; Thorgusen, S.R.; Regelbrugge, J.C.; Weise, D.; Lee, C. 2003. Modeling seasonal changes in live fuel moisture and equivalent water thickness using a cumulative water balance index. Remote Sensing of Environment. 88: 442–452.

Finney, M.A. 1998. FARSITE: Fire Area Simulator-model development and evaluation. Res. Pap. RMRS-RP-4. Fort Collins, CO: U.S. Department of Agriculture, Forest Service, Rocky Mountain Research Station. 47 p.

Finney, M.A. 2001. Design of regular landscape fuel treatment patterns for modifying fire growth and behavior. Forest Science. 47: 219–228.

Finney, M.A. 2002. Fire growth using minimum travel time methods. Canadian Journal of Forest Research. 32: 1420-1424.

Finney, M.A. 2006. An overview of FlamMap fire modeling capabilities. In: Andrews, P.L.; Butler, B.W., eds. Proceedings, Fuels management—how to measure success conference. Proc. RMRS-P-41. Fort Collins, CO: U.S. Department of Agriculture, Forest Service, Rocky Mountain Research Station: 213–220.

Fons, W.L. 1946. Analysis of fire spread in light fuels. Journal of Agricultural Research. 72: 93–121.

Frandsen, W.H.; Andrews, P.L. 1979. Fire behavior in nonuniform fuels. Res. Pap. INT-RP-232. Ogden, UT: U.S. Department of Agriculture, Forest Service, Intermountain Forest and Range Experiment Station. 34 p.

Franklin J. 1997. Forest Service southern California mapping project: Santa Monica Mountains National Recreation Area. [San Diego, CA]: [San Diego State University]; final report; U.S. Department of Agriculture, Forest Service contract 53-91S8-3-TM45. 11 p.

French, I.A.; Anderson, D.H.; Catchpole, E.A. 1990. Graphical simulation of bushfire spread. Mathematical Computer Modelling. 13: 67–71.

Green, D.G. 1983. Shapes of simulated fires in discrete fuels. Ecological Modeling. 20: 21-32.

Green, D.G.; Tridgell, A.; Gill, M.A. 1990. Interactive simulation of bushfires in heterogeneous fuels. Mathematical and Computer Modelling. 13: 57–66.

Greig-Smith, P. 1983. Quantitative plant ecology. 3rd ed. Berkeley, CA: University of California Press. 374 p.

Hanson, H.P.; Bradley, M.M.; Bossert, J.E.; Linn, R.R.; Younker, L.W. 2000. The potential and promise of physics-based wildfire simulation. Environmental Science and Policy. 3: 171–172.

Hargrove, W.W.; Gardner, R.H.; Turner, M.G.; Romme, W.H.; Despain, D.G. 2000. Simulating fire patterns in heterogeneous landscapes. Ecological Modeling. 135: 243-263.

Keeley, J.E.; Fotheringham, C.J.; Morais, M. 1999. Reexamining fire suppression impacts on brushland fire regimes. Science. 284: 1829–1832.

Kourtz, P.H.; O'Regan, W.G. 1971. A model for a small forest fire, to simulate burned and burning areas for use in a detection model. Forest Science. 17: 163–169.

Linn, R.R. 1997. A transport model for prediction of wildfire behavior. Las Cruces, NM: New Mexico State University, Los Alamos National Laboratory. 195 p. Ph.D. dissertation.

Linn, R.R.; Reisner, J.; Colman, J.J.; Winterkamp, J. 2002. Studying wildfire behavior using FIRETEC. International Journal of Wildland Fire. 11: 233–246.

Morais, M. 2001. Comparing spatially explicit models of fire spread through chaparral fuels: a new algorithm based upon the Rothermel Fire spread Equation. Santa Barbara, CA: University of California. 66 p. M.A. thesis.

Moritz, M.A.; Keeley, J.E.; Johnson, E.A.; Schaffner, A.A. 2004. Testing a basic assumption of shrubland fire management: How important is fuel age? Frontiers in Ecology and the Environment. 2: 67–72.

Moritz, M.A.; Morais, M.E.; Summerell, L.A.; Carlson, J.M.; Doyle, J. 2005. Wildfires, complexity, and highly optimized tolerance. Proceedings of the National Academy of Sciences of the United States of America. 102(50): 17912–17917.

Moritz, M.A.; Stephens, S.L. [In press]. Fire and sustainability: considerations for California's altered future climate. Climatic Change.

Nelson, R.M.; Adkins, C.W. 1988. A dimensionless correlation for the spread of wind-driven fires. Canadian Journal of Forest Research. 18: 391–397.

Ntaimo, L.; Zeigler, B.P.; Vasconcelos, M.J.; Khargharia, B. 2004. Forest fire spread and suppression in DEVS. SIMULATION: Transactions of the Society for Modeling and Simulation International. 80(10): 479–500.

Perry, G.L.W.; Sparrow, A.D.; Owens, I.F. 1999. A GIS-supported model for the simulation of the spatial structure of wildland fire, Cass Basin, New Zealand. Journal of Applied Ecology. 36: 502–518.

Peterson, S.H.; Goldstein, N.C.; Clark, M.L.; Halligan, K.Q.; Schneider, P.; Dennison, P.E.; Roberts, D.A. 2005. Sensitivity analysis of the 2003 Simi Wildfire Event. In: Xie, Y.; Brown, D.G., eds. Proceedings of the 8th international conference on geocomputation. Ann Arbor, MI. http://www.geocomputation. org/2005/index.html. (25 July 2008).

Peterson, S.H.; Roberts, D.A.; Dennison, P.E. [In press]. Mapping live fuel moisture with MODIS data: a multiple regression approach. Remote Sensing of Environment.

Pitts, W.M. 1991. Wind effects on fires. Progress Energy Combustion Science. 17: 83–134.

Prometheus. 2008. The Canadian Wildland Fire Growth Model (CWFGM). Prometheus ver. 5.1.8. http://www.firegrowthmodel.com/index.cfm. (25 July 2008).

Richards, G.D. 1990. An elliptical growth model of forest fire fronts and its numerical solution. International Journal for Numerical Methods in Engineering. 30: 1163-1179.

Roberts, D.A.; Dennison, P.E.; Peterson, S.H.; Sweeney, S.; Rechel, J. 2006. Evaluation of AVIRIS and MODIS measures of live fuel moisture and fuel condition in a shrubland ecosystem in southern California. Journal of Geophysical Research—Biogeosciences. 111: G04S02.

Rothermel, R.C. 1972. A mathematical model for predicting fire spread in wildland fuels. Res. Pap. INT-RP-115. Ogden, UT: U.S. Department of Agriculture, Forest Service, Intermountain Forest and Range Experiment Station. 40 p.

Rothermel, R.C. 1983. How to predict the spread and intensity of forest and range fires. Gen. Tech. Rep. INT-GTR-143. Ogden, UT: U.S. Department of Agriculture, Forest Service, Intermountain Forest and Range Experiment Station. 161 p.

Rothermel, R.C. 1991. Predicting the behavior and size of crown fires in the northern Rocky Mountains. Res. Pap. INT-RP-438. Ogden, UT: U.S. Department of Agriculture, Forest Service, Intermountain Forest and Range Experiment Station. 48 p.

Rothermel, R.C.; Wilson, R.A.; Morris, G.A.; Sackett, S.S. 1986. Modeling moisture content of fine dead wildland fuels: Input to the BEHAVE fire prediction system. Res. Pap. INT-RP-359. Ogden, UT: U.S. Department of Agriculture, Forest Service, Intermountain Forest and Range Experiment Station. 61 p.

Vasconcelos, M.J.; Guertin, D.P. 1992. FIREMAP—simulation of fire growth with a geographic information system. International Journal of Wildland Fire. 2: 87–96.

Weber, R.O. 1991. Modeling fire spread through fuel beds. Progress in Energy and Combustion Science. 17: 67–82.

Weise, D.R.; Regelbrugge, J.C. 1997. Recent chaparral fuel modeling efforts. Resource Management: The Fire Element (Newsletter of the California Fuels Committee). Summer 1997 issue. 1 p.

Williams, F.A. 1976. Mechanisms of fire spread. In: Proceedings, 16th symposium on combustion. Pittsburgh, PA: The Combustion Institute: 1281–1294.

Yassemi, S.; Dragićević, S.; Schmidt, M. 2008. Design and implementation of an integrated GIS-based cellular automata model to characterize forest fire behaviour. Ecological Modelling. 210: 71–84.

www.ingramcontent.com/pod-product-compliance
Lightning Source LLC
Chambersburg PA
CBHW081123280526
45787CB00007B/2952